# FAMILY CONSEQUENCES OF CHILDREN'S DISABILITIES

# FAMILY CONSEQUENCES OF CHILDREN'S DISABILITIES

DENNIS HOGAN

With the collaboration of Michael E. Msall, Frances K. Goldscheider,
Carrie L. Shandra, and Roger C. Avery

A Volume in the American Sociological Association's
Rose Series in Sociology

Russell Sage Foundation • New York

**Library of Congress Cataloging-in-Publication Data**

Hogan, Dennis.
    Family consequences of children's disabilities / Dennis Hogan.
    p. cm.
    Includes bibliographical references and index.
    ISBN 978-0-87154-457-5 (pbk. : alk. paper) – ISBN 978-1-61044-773-7 (ebook)
        1. Parents of children with disabilities–United States.    2. Parents of
children with disabilities–Services for–United States.    3. Children with
disabilities–United States.    4. Children with disabilities–Services for–United
States.    I. Title.
    HQ759.913.H64 2012
    362.408–dc23        2011053535

Text design by Suzanne Nichols.

RUSSELL SAGE FOUNDATION
112 East 64th Street, New York, New York 10065
10 9 8 7 6 5 4 3 2 1

# The Russell Sage Foundation

The Russell Sage Foundation, one of the oldest of America's general purpose foundations, was established in 1907 by Mrs. Margaret Olivia Sage for "the improvement of social and living conditions in the United States." The Foundation seeks to fulfill this mandate by fostering the development and dissemination of knowledge about the country's political, social, and economic problems. While the Foundation endeavors to assure the accuracy and objectivity of each book it publishes, the conclusions and interpretations in Russell Sage Foundation publications are those of the authors and not of the Foundation, its Trustees, or its staff. Publication by Russell Sage, therefore, does not imply Foundation endorsement.

# Previous Volumes in the Series

*Social Movements in the World-System: The Politics of Crisis and Transformation*
Dawn Wiest and Jackie Smith

*They Say Cut Back, We Say Fight Back! Welfare Activism in an Era of Retrenchment*
Ellen Reese

*Trust in Schools: A Core Resource for Improvement*
Anthony S. Bryk and Barbara Schneider

# ═ Forthcoming Titles ═

*Embedded Dependency: Minority Set-Asides, Black Entrepreneurs, and the White Construction Monopoly*
Deirdre Royster

*Family Relationships Across the Generations*
Judith A. Seltzer and Suzanne M. Bianchi

*Global Order and the Historical Structures of Daral-Islam*
Mohammed A. Bamyeh

*The Logic of Terrorism: A Comparative Study*
Jeff Goodwin

*The Long Shadow: Family Background, Disadvantaged Urban Youth, and the Transition to Adulthood*
Karl Alexander, Doris Entwisle, and Linda Olson

*Repressive Injustice: Political and Social Processes in the Massive Incarceration of African Americans*
Pamela E. Oliver and James E. Yocum

# The Rose Series in Sociology

THE AMERICAN Sociological Association's Rose Series in Sociology publishes books that integrate knowledge and address controversies from a sociological perspective. Books in the Rose Series are at the forefront of sociological knowledge. They are lively and often involve timely and fundamental issues on significant social concerns. The series is intended for broad dissemination throughout sociology, across social science and other professional communities, and to policy audiences. The series was established in 1967 by a bequest to ASA from Arnold and Caroline Rose to support innovations in scholarly publishing.

LEE CLARKE
JUDITH GERSON
LAUREN KRIVO
PAUL MCLEAN
PATRICIA ROOS

EDITORS

*For Matt Hogan and his family*

# Contents

# ═ About the Authors ═

**Dennis Hogan** is Robert E. Turner Distinguished Professor of Population Studies and professor of sociology at Brown University.

**Roger C. Avery** was associate professor of research in population studies at Brown University, now retired.

**Frances K. Goldscheider** is professor emerita in sociology and population studies at Brown University.

**Michael E. Msall** is professor of pediatrics and section chief, developmental and behavioral pediatrics, Department of Medicine, University of Chicago.

**Carrie L. Shandra** is assistant professor of sociology at Hofstra University.

# = Preface =

M Y INITIAL interest in studying the family consequences of children's disabilities was rooted in personal experience, as my brother Matt had Down syndrome. I first began to look into the possibility of a demographic study of disability among children in 1993 but could find no population-level data on potentially disabling medical conditions. The situation changed with the passage of the Americans with Disabilities Act and efforts of the federal statistical system to collect information on the disability status of children as well as of adults. By 1996, the National Health Interview Survey on Disability had collected the necessary data, including crucial information on limitations in daily activities, that made possible a demographic study of disabilities among children. Subsequent data collection efforts by the federal statistical system provided greatly enriched information about children's disabilities, the lives of their family members, and family functioning. My friend and colleague Bob Weller alerted me to these data collection efforts, shared with me his own research on children with disabilities, and provided encouragement to continue this research.

My fifteen years of research on children with disabilities and their families was only possible because of generous financial support from the National Institutes of Health, private foundations, and Brown University. The National Institute of Child Health and Human Development (NICHD) provided an initial project development grant (NICHD #1 R03 HD35376, "The Demography of Child Disability and Rehabilitation"). In collaboration with Frances Goldscheider and Michael Msall, I was awarded a five-year grant (NICHD #5 U01 HD37614) for the project "Child Disability and the Family." This grant supported our participation in the NICHD Network on Family and Child Well-Being, which met several times each year from 1999 to 2005. The Office of the Secretary for Policy Evaluation at the National Institutes of Health and the National Center for Medical Rehabilitation Research provided supplements to this NICHD grant to support development of new methods for demographic analysis of children with disabilities using population survey and census data. I especially thank V. Jeffrey Evans and Louis

Quatrano of the NICHD for their encouragement and support of this new line of research. This research also received generous support from the William T. Grant Foundation and the Spencer Foundation to investigate how parents raise children with disabilities, and the transitions of children with disabilities from adolescence to adulthood. Brown University provided a timely Richard B. Salomon Faculty Research Award, "The Family Consequences of Child Disability," which supported semistructured interviews of parents of children with disabilities at the Children's Rehabilitation Center.

In addition to this financial support, the research received substantial support in terms of space and services from the Population Studies and Training Center and the Department of Sociology at Brown University. Release time from teaching was provided by the Robert E. Turner Distinguished Professorship in Population Studies, which I am fortunate to hold. The outstanding intellectual climate at Brown University offered a supportive environment for this research while challenging me to defend the idea of population-based studies of children with disabilities and to address the inadequacies of my initial efforts. In particular, the extensive comments of Michael White and Phil Brown on an earlier version of this manuscript were quite helpful. I also thank Michele Wise, Doug Brown, and Bob and Jean Weller for sharing their experiences as parents of children with disabilities.

During the course of my research on the study of children's disabilities and family life, I have worked with faculty colleagues and a succession of graduate students to plan the focus and analysis of the data and to discuss and debate the results. I begin by thanking Michael Msall, MD, for his mentorship and collaboration on the survey measurement of children's disabilities with population-based information on medical impairments, diagnoses, and services. His partnership was critical for the translation of population-level data and clinical information into a coherent framework for the study of children with disabilities, as is recognized in his coauthorship of chapter 2 on the analysis of disability.

Frances Goldscheider was my colleague and collaborator on the research on the family consequences of children with disabilities. She provided the necessary encouragement to keep me focused on the effects of a child with disabilities on the family lives and careers of mothers and fathers. She was also a font of ideas and a faithful critic. Fran originated the idea of matching the National Health Interview Survey and the National Survey of Family Growth to produce a unique data resource for research on the consequences of children's disabilities on mothers' lives. She also was a strong advocate of the semi-structured interviews at the Children's Rehabilitation Center. We planned a much different version of this book together, and Fran provided extensive comments on several early chapter drafts. She also collaborated in analyzing data and commenting on the write-up of chapter 3, as indicated by her coauthorship of that chapter. While we ultimately did not coauthor this book, I owe her a tremendous debt of gratitude.

Roger Avery provided important assistance in the analysis of survey and census data, with particular expertise in unraveling the procedural and coding mysteries of these data; he is coauthor of chapter 2. Thomas Wells brought considerable statistical expertise and craftsmanship to the measurement of disability among children using alternative sources of population data and to the study of pathways to adulthood that are followed by children with disabilities. With Gary Sandefur, Tom was instrumental in our early work on the pathways to adulthood of adolescents with disabilities. Gary is a tremendous collaborator and friend, and I greatly enjoyed our work together.

I worked with Michelle Rogers at the outset of this research; she made particular contributions to analyses that use the National Health Interview Surveys. The collaboration with Michelle led to early publication success (with Michael Msall) on the subject of the disadvantageous family origins of children with disabilities and demonstrated some of the family consequences of children with disabilities, highlighting the costs of medical and rehabilitation services.

Jennifer Park, Carrie Spearin, and Julie Lima undertook the agonizing process of matching the 1993 National Health Interview Survey and the National Survey of Family Growth to study the impact of children with disabilities on the lives of their mothers.

Maryhelen D'Ottavi MacInnes, along with Catherine Stiff Andrzejewski and Brian Mayer, conducted the in-depth interviews of parents of children with disabilities and handled the complex tasks of transcription and coding. Their work on this aspect of the project was superb and contributed immeasurably to this study. I also thank Michael Spoerri for facilitating access to the families at the Children's Rehabilitation Center. Thanks are especially due to these families for their willingness to share their personal and family experiences raising their children with disabilities.

Julia Drew brought her commitment to the study of persons with disability to the tabulations of the insurance coverage, health access, health care, and medical home of children with disabilities. Carrie Shandra brought her superb research skills to investigate the parenting of children with disabilities and the educational attainments of children with disabilities, and coauthored papers on these subjects. She is coauthor of chapter 5, which focuses on parenting children with disabilities.

I was fortunate to have this book accepted by the American Sociological Association's Rose Monograph Series. The Rose Series provides funding to support a three-quarter day seminar on the book manuscript in its early stages. This seminar, held at the Russell Sage Foundation, was an extraordinary experience that brought together editors from the State University of New York–Stony Brook, who edited other volumes in the Rose Monograph Series, with resident scholars at the Russell Sage Foundation, especially Thomas DiPrete, Shelley Lundgren, and Sara McLanahan, who came to the seminar at my request. The many suggestions of these superb scholars provided me with a wealth of ideas for the manuscript's revision. The most valuable aspect of being part of the Rose Monograph Series, however, was the unparalleled opportunity to work with Series Editor Naomi Rosenthal, under whose guidance I took a manuscript that was written for a statistical audience and transformed it into a manuscript that is much more accessible to the general reader. This was a new and valuable experience for me; it is a skill that I will employ in my future writing.

Kelley Smith provided thorough editing of multiple drafts of this revised manuscript, greatly improving its adherence to principles of written English and its clarity. Kelley's own research experience complemented her superb editorial skills in improving this final product.

Finally, I wish to acknowledge Suzanne Nichols, editor at the Russell Sage Foundation, and the reviewers, Suzanne Bianchi and Andrew Cherlin, whose directions for revision brought this manuscript to a much better organized and more intelligent book.

I wish to thank Mary Fennell for her encouragement. Without Mary's support, particularly during a number of health crises that left me discouraged to continue, this project would not have been completed. I thank, too, my friend and mentor John Anderson for his continuing efforts to keep me focused, on track, and productive.

Finally, I want to thank my parents, my brothers and sisters, and their families, who provided the example and inspiration for this study. While population data provide an average picture and do not represent the experiences of any particular family, the research questions asked and the issues examined in this study are rooted in the experiences of my family and those of many other families of children with disabilities. My sister, Sally Poesch, was incredibly helpful through her careful reading of this manuscript and suggestions for its improvement. I am eleven years older than my brother Matt and did not see his daily life at home as he reached adolescence and early adulthood, except for frequent short family visits. Sally's insights into this time in Matt's life, and his later residential placement in a magnificent facility for special-needs people, provided family insights that I lack.

# = Chapter 1 =

## Families' Experiences with Children's Disabilities

MORE THAN one-eighth of all families with children in the United States include at least one child under age eighteen who has been diagnosed as having a disability. Nearly all of those children live with their families. Their disabilities range from mild (for example, asthma that limits participation in sports) to severe (such as cerebral palsy with extensive neurological complications). All told, 6.5 million American school-age children have a disability, and for 4.3 million of them, the disability is seriously limiting. This book is about how American families respond to the challenges of raising children with disabilities, and how these challenges affect those families.

### Four Families

The following four families' experiences illustrate what can happen when a child has a disability.

### *Jake's Family*

Thomas and Sandra are the parents of Jake, age ten, and Katie, age seven. They are a white, middle-class family, and Thomas works at a professional job. They have sufficient income to meet all basic family needs. It was clear early on that Jake was different from other children. As a baby and young toddler, Jake would not meet his parents' eyes, was seldom interested in others unless they were giving something he wanted, and ignored children his age. By his second birthday, Jake still did not say words. After months of telling themselves he was just developing late, Thomas and Sandra took Jake to a major medical center for tests. They were stunned when the doctors told them Jake had autism. They knew little about autism—its symptoms, its progression, or its treatment. They went home and consulted library materials and the

Internet. They looked into medical sites, material by educators, and advocacy groups, and they had conversations with other parents. And they looked to themselves to consider what they could and would do to best help Jake.

After much discussion, Sandra agreed to a strategy that Thomas had been advocating. Rather than undertaking medical treatments, intensive expert behavioral interventions, unproven special diets, and the like, they decided to work with Jake at home to help him participate in family, social, and educational roles. Based on what they had learned, they realized that they would need to provide an exceptionally calm home environment, patiently encouraging slow step-by-step progress in self-care, play, speaking, and using skills as an integral part of functioning, rather than simply repeating these skills again and again until they were mastered for practical use.

Above all, they wanted to emphasize overwhelming family love in Jake's life. Sandra quit her job to become the primary caregiver for Jake. However, although her commitment to Jake is strong, her time at home has been far from easy. Thomas sometimes comes home from work to discover Sandra at wits' end—frustrated, angry, and far from calm. When this happens, Thomas is able to take a fresh approach with Jake in order to help settle the entire family. To take part in the day-to-day challenges of raising Jake, Thomas sometimes works at home, and he stays home evenings and weekends so that he can provide some relief for Sandra as Jake's primary caregiver.

Within a few years of the initial diagnosis, Jake began to interact with family and then with age-mates. He was able to enter kindergarten on schedule. However, the central city public schools were unable to provide the support Jake needed. Because Sandra had stopped working in order to be with Jake at home, the family could not afford to pay for a special school for children with disabilities. Moreover, they were committed to mainstreaming Jake in a regular school. The costs of private schools for Jake were prohibitive, and these schools typically do not have mainstream programs. Thomas and Sandra ended up moving to an affluent suburb that they do not like, but where the public school can give Jake the educational supports he needs. He is now doing grade-level academic work and has made some friends, including friends without disabilities. But Thomas worries that as he becomes a teenager, Jake will lose friends who begin to consider him "different" or even "weird." Thomas has no sense of how Jake might function in the adult world; for the moment, he's focused on getting Jake through school, keeping him involved with peers, and enabling him with the range of skills needed for participation in adult life.

## Brandon's Family

Brandon, age five, is the son of Karen and Gregory. They are a working-class family who live in a rural town. Brandon has had multiple severely disabling medical conditions since birth. He has pressure on the brain caused by the premature closing of the growth plates in the head. This condition can be corrected by surgery, but Brandon did not get the surgery until age three, after some of the worst damage to his verbal and motor functions had occurred, because, in the words of his parents, his previous neurologist was "an idiot" who has since lost his medical license. Since birth, Brandon has had a digestive condition that causes projectile vomiting. He has failed to thrive; at five years of age, he is only 40 inches tall and weighs only 33 pounds—both measurements are lower than 99 percent of all children of the same age. Brandon also suffers from epilepsy, asthma, and severe anger and aggression.

Karen says she is the only one who can take care of Brandon. This is her full-time job, and having to fight for him is central to her identity. Brandon receives physical and occupational therapy at a medical center four days per week and does therapeutic horseback riding one day a week. Karen coordinates his medical appointments with his part-time special education program and makes sure he gets to the right place at the right time. He is mainstreamed in a preschool program with an individual education plan that provides additional physical and occupational therapies. To attend school, Brandon needs personal aides to help with his diet, eating, and digestion; to work buttons and zippers; and to assist with toileting and frequent incontinence. Karen reports that she is constantly tired and often lacks sufficient sleep. The only free time she has is after Brandon goes to sleep, when she does crafts and watches movies on television.

Karen says that alternative at-home care arrangements cannot provide the same kind of care that she gives Brandon; as a result, she and Gregory have no social life outside their home. Karen has a brother and sister who live next door but are of no help. If she gets too sick to care for Brandon, her mother will help. Karen also says she cannot rely on Gregory for Brandon's care—he loses patience and becomes very angry, especially at Brandon's violent outbursts. Karen is afraid that, if left alone with Brandon, Gregory would physically abuse him. She does not let Gregory provide care, even if it is just for a short trip to the store—she says it is just too dangerous.

Karen became unemployed the day after she learned she was pregnant with Brandon. She was sterilized after Brandon was born so that she could devote herself entirely to his needs. Gregory, however, wants to have another child. Though they were married just six months before Brandon was born, Karen and Gregory are no longer intimate; their marriage is in danger. Karen thinks it is possible Gregory will abandon them.

Karen and Gregory have been financially ruined by their reduced income and the special costs of Brandon's disabilities. Gregory works at night for minimum wage. Karen tries to supplement their income with Tupperware sales at home. Karen is diabetic and believes that her own health has been harmed by Brandon's needs and lack of attention to herself. Gregory and Karen declared bankruptcy because of unpaid medical bills and credit card debts. They are chronically unable to pay their monthly bills. They do not always know if they will have food to eat, so they have reduced their consumption of meats and fresh fruits. On some days, they eat only two meals.

## Christina's Family

In August of 1992, Christina, the second of three daughters, was born to Todd and Michele. Christina's sisters did not have disabilities. After seeming to develop normally for the first few months, Christina began to show deficits in her development. As Christina got older, she was unable to crawl or walk. She did not speak words, although she used her verbal abilities to communicate. Physicians diagnosed her as having a global developmental delay or a form of cerebral palsy. Over time, Christina's parents became convinced this diagnosis was incorrect: Christina was bright-eyed and could understand, but she could not speak; she enjoyed the world around her and liked to participate; she wanted to walk but was unable to do so. She was not able to eat, bathe, or dress by herself and could not be toilet trained. She had difficulty digesting food and was diagnosed with gastroesophageal reflux disease. Christina also had scoliosis, or curvature of the spine, and a significant seizure disorder.

Michele and her husband kept pushing the doctors for a more comprehensive diagnosis, with no success. Finally, as a result of their online investigation of medical conditions, they began to suspect Christina had Rett syndrome, a neurological disorder affecting only females. Rett syndrome is characterized by deterioration in function over time, and survival rates decline after age ten. Pneumonia is often followed by death. Because the condition is very rare (fewer than one in ten thousand girls have it) and the United States did not have its first diagnosed case of Rett syndrome until 1983, their physicians doubted their suspicions. Still, Michele and Todd insisted that their neurologist order the diagnostic test, and at age ten, Christina was finally diagnosed with Rett syndrome.

Christina was able to go to a public school for special-needs children. Her father and mother both continued to work to support Christina and her sisters; Michele's job provided better health insurance. But one of the parents also had to see Christina off to school (on a special bus) and meet her when she came back home; the state did not allow her sisters to do this. Michele, who holds an important administrative position, was able to negotiate flexible hours with her employer so that she could handle arrangements for Christina's schooling, doctor appointments, and special care needs.

Both parents and children were actively involved in Christina's care and enjoyed involving her in family activities. Todd and Michele retrofitted their house to handle Christina's needs with wheelchairs, an electric lift to bring her up and down the stairs, a wheel-in shower, and a ramp to get her into the house. Many of these accommodations would only work as long as her parents could lift and carry her. In anticipation of not being able to do this, the family installed a pulley and lift system to move Christina between rooms.

Michele's insurance covered Christina's medical care. The family received financial assistance from the state-administered Katie Beckett Program (which helps middle-income families afford the substantial expenses of keeping a child with severe disabilities at home). This included financial help for the purchase of a succession of wheelchairs as Christina grew larger, the pulley and lift system, special foods, and diapers. The schools mobilized resources so that Christina could continue her schooling. Michele says that the family feels good about what they did—they not only coped, but also thrived, creating a loving and supportive home centered on Christina's needs. Because of these supports, there was adequate income for all family needs.

After her twelfth birthday, Christina began to have recurring respiratory problems and spent many weeks repeatedly hospitalized. Finally, after she turned thirteen, Christina developed severe pneumonia and succumbed to a cascade of medical problems. While Christina's situation had been dire, her death was not expected. Her father had just left on an international business trip, and after arriving at his destination airport caught the next flight home. As her husband was still en route to the hospital, Michele was left to face the situation alone. The hospital's neurologist was blunt with Michele, pronouncing Christina brain dead after only a brief neurological assessment, and recommended that they take her off life support. He was not well known to Michele and her family and made no attempt to sit and speak with

Michele, offer any kind words, or even offer his condolence. Michele felt the neurologist lacked sympathy, as well as any sort of understanding as to what Christina meant to the family. This lack of compassion made Michele feel very angry. More than a year later, Michele still feels that way.

Today, the family has begun to adjust and to do some things that were impossible when Christina was with them. Michele has returned to her job during regular business hours, and the family is very involved with the Rett Foundation, working to increase awareness of Rett syndrome as a way to honor Christina's life. They've taken a vacation, and their oldest daughter is beginning to look at colleges, both parents visiting campuses with her. Michele carries a small book of prayers and poems with Christina's picture and holy card. But the hole in their family life is gaping. It continues to be unsettling, sad, and difficult to adjust to the loss of such a focal family member.

### Derek's Family

Derek, an African American four-year-old, was playing with his cousin on the sidewalk in front of his public housing apartment; there were no parks or playgrounds in the neighborhood. A person riding a dirt bike rounded the corner at high speed and swerved onto the sidewalk to avoid a speed bump, hitting Derek and a telephone pole. The bike bounced off the pole and landed on Derek's head. Derek's mother panicked and needed neighbors to help call for an ambulance. Derek spent one month in a local pediatric hospital, two weeks of which were in critical care. At first, his chance of survival was touch and go. After Derek's situation stabilized, it became clear that Derek's brain injury had paralyzed his left side. Medicaid covered the cost of Derek's initial care and rehabilitation therapy. Now he is covered by state medical insurance for persons on Social Security Disability Insurance.

Derek was sent to a university rehabilitation hospital that was a seventy-minute drive away from home. The doctors were not optimistic about even a partial recovery. But Derek's mother, Alicia, saw him as a fighter determined to overcome his disability. In fact, Derek made a remarkable physical recovery, and one year later he is able to walk with leg braces (although he tends to fall over) and to use his arm. He needs help with bathing and dressing but otherwise can care for himself. However, Derek's physical recovery has not been matched by cognitive and mental health recovery. While his disability is not severe, it is likely Derek will require special education in a regular school. The biggest problem for Alicia is that Derek's personality has changed—he now angers easily and turns violent; Alicia says "he is mean." She will not leave him alone with his younger brothers (ages two and four) out of fear that he will hurt them. He cannot be taken out to the homes of others or to play with his cousins. His mother keeps him inside where he is "safe" and where his anger cannot result in him hurting another child.

Alicia did not complete high school after giving birth to Derek when she was age seventeen. Alicia has never worked for pay and has not been married. Derek's father has never supported Alicia and her family financially, even after Derek's injury, but he is "around." He stayed with Derek for the first week when he was in the rehabilitation hospital. He sometimes takes care of the younger children while Alicia brings Derek to therapy. Alicia seems satisfied with the level of his involvement in their lives.

However, Alicia mainly relies on her own family for help with child care and for sharing the costs of basic family necessities such as heat, food, and clothing. Even with their help, Alicia and her children live in poverty in shabby and cramped public housing. An aunt who lives next door typically takes care of the younger children when Alicia needs to take Derek to tests and treatments and watches all of the children when Alicia needs to go out.

Alicia deals with Derek's needs and is a good mother to her other children. But she remains angry about one thing—the driver of the dirt bike was initially charged with reckless driving resulting in serious injury, but the charges were dropped when he told the police about another dirt bike driver who illegally possessed a gun, thus getting off the hook by providing information about another, unrelated crime.

## Family-Centered Care

The United States depends on families like those of Jake, Brandon, Christina, and Derek to assume the extraordinary responsibilities of raising children with disabilities, although as a nation, we have made an unprecedented commitment to emancipate persons with disabilities. The Individuals with Disabilities Education Acts (IDEA) of 1975 and 1997 guarantee children with disabilities an education that maximizes their full potential and that is provided in a school setting most closely approximating that of other children. The Americans with Disabilities Act (ADA) of 1990 emphasizes the potential for all persons with disabilities to participate fully in American life, with appropriate medical care, rehabilitation, and helpful social and physical environments. But these national policies expect that children with disabilities will reside at home and that parents will provide them with medical care, provide them with access to an education that maximizes their potential, and equip them for adult life.

This national strategy of family-centered responsibility works, to a large extent. When a child with a disability is born into a family, most parents do everything they can to promote that child's well-being and life chances. This book focuses on what parents do when they have a child with a disability and how this affects them and other children in the family. Specialists who care for children with disabilities know there are costs and consequences for many families raising children with disabilities, and the families of children with disabilities are all too familiar with many of those. As the literature makes clear, a family's experience of a child's disability depends on that child's medical conditions, the severity of those conditions, and how those conditions affect the child's abilities and everyday activities.

## The Population Approach

This book uses case studies like those of Jake, Brandon, Christina, and Derek. My approach is unique in that I also use information representative of American families raising children with disabilities to portray commonalities and variety among families, describe the added responsibilities and parenting challenges they undertake, and investigate the consequences for family life and family members.

The population approach involves the use of representative survey data that refer to all American families raising children with disabilities. This approach means that I can study families whose children have what appear to be relatively mild disabilities, rather than paying attention to just families of children with more serious or severe disabilities. By using information from the Census and seven national surveys, I can provide a comprehensive picture of the disability status of children and the wide variety of family situations and impacts on the family. In this way, I present a portrait of all American children with disabilities and their families, and it is possible to examine how they compare to families whose children do not have disabilities. The population approach also permits me to examine how children's disabilities affect the situations of all types of families—those that are poor and those that are economically secure, households with one parent or two, families with health insurance and families that lack insurance, and minority families, as well as families who are in the American majority.

A population approach is useful in other ways, as well. For example, there are children with disabilities who may never obtain necessary specialized medical or rehabilitation care and thus do not appear in published clinical studies. A population approach can identify children with unmet needs for specialized care and the problems their parents encounter in getting this care. In contrast, some children may have received appropriate specialized care and modifications to their environments so that they are able to do all daily activities and can participate fully in all age-appropriate roles. These success stories may have been missed in prior studies focused exclusively on children who have ongoing disabilities.

Using information from representative national data on families and more detailed interviews with parents of children with disabilities, this book shows that there are numerous consequences for families raising children with disabilities, many of which are not favorable. Parents of children with disabilities divorce more often than parents of children without disabilities and sometimes change their plans about how many children they will have. Family life is almost always reorganized so that disabled children can receive all the care they need. Against the trend for women to be in the workforce, mothers of disabled children are more likely to be full-time homemakers with primary caregiving responsibilities, and fathers are more likely to work longer hours, work at two jobs, or continue working beyond retirement age to support the family. This return to traditional family roles reduces income at a time when families face unparalleled expenses. Brothers and sisters of children with disabilities thus grow up in families with more expenses and fewer resources. To cover the needs of a disabled child, parents sometimes allocate a smaller share of those resources to their non-disabled children than they would if they did not have a disabled child.

The population approach helps to assess whether media accounts of extreme actions of parents of children with disabilities reflect the reality of how these families function. Most people have seen or heard media coverage of parents who avoid taking care of their disabled child. For example, in one New England town, news sources reported on a woman who had a prenatal test to determine if her fetus had Down syndrome and was told the baby would be healthy. However, there was a mix-up in the lab work, and she gave birth to a child with Down syndrome. Immediately at birth, she placed her child in a permanent residential facility and supposedly used some of the money gained in her lawsuit against the laboratory to remodel her kitchen.

Such stories are outrageous and get considerable public attention. But the fact is that such instances are extremely rare and do not even show up in population data. Overblown media attention to such stories does a public disservice by distracting from the real sacrifices made by nearly all parents of children with disabilities. The purpose of this book is to demonstrate to Americans and our policymakers that the actual situations of most families of children with disabilities are quite different.

I have given many professional and public lectures on these findings. Many members of the audiences are often astonished. This book will likely stun readers unfamiliar with these families' challenges, but it is essential for a broader public understanding of the struggles and needs of families with children with disabilities. While the findings of this study may not surprise parents of children with disabilities, such parents may be surprised by the extent to which my findings apply to parents of children with all types of disabilities, not just children who have the same medical conditions as their own child. This book should reassure parents of children with disabilities that they are not alone.

## The Constantly Changing Lives of Parents and Children

While disability associated with old age tends to be a progressive process, this is not the case for many children with disabilities: their disabilities can diminish, disappear, or worsen as they grow to adult ages. They may be able to participate in schools, but in other contexts, such as work, they may not have as many opportunities.

This means that over time, changes occur in their capabilities and needs, affecting their ability to perform daily tasks in life (for example, feeding, dressing, and bathing themselves) and to participate in social life (going to school, making friends, and working at a job). The age of children with disabilities is implicated in this process, especially in regard to age-appropriate activities. This is best thought of as a dynamic process in which the life of the child with a disability, and changes in the disability, are linked to the lives of others in the family, and the lives of all family members are linked to each other. The lives of children with disabilities are, in turn, affected by what their families do.

I use life course theory to study children with disabilities and the consequences of disability for parents, brothers and sisters, and the family (Elder, Johnson, and Crosnoe 2003). Life course theory regards the lives of individuals from birth to death (or some portion thereof) as being structured by the unique historical times in which they live, the social institutions they encounter, and family and community environments. Life course theory also directs attention to how experiences at one age influence options and experiences at later ages; when individuals follow an established life course pattern they are said to follow a life course pathway. A key element of the life course is individual choice—that is, based on prior experiences, their interpretation of those experiences, and what they see as their (constrained) options, individuals exercise agency and can affect their own life courses.

Life course theory helps situate the families of children with disabilities and directs attention to specific aspects of the life courses of family members. The families studied here are historically unique—they are the first families raising children under new government policies that promote the inclusion of persons with disability in all aspects of life. For these families, the option of placing their young children in an institutional setting is largely absent. No matter how seriously disabled a child may be, national policy expects that families will provide comprehensive care.

There have been some institutional changes intended to help parents in this regard. Medical services are supposed to be available to meet the needs of children with disabilities. Yet, as this study shows, the organization of medical practice, diagnoses, and care delivery is often unsatisfactory. This situation is further exacerbated by private and public insurance options and limitations in coverage. Schools are mandated to provide medical and rehabilitation assistance free of charge to enable a child with a disability to participate in regular schooling to the extent possible. However, school access to such support only occurs when funding allows, and parents often need to fight with schools for correct diagnoses and necessary services.

Parents of older children with disabilities face significant challenges finding suitable employment for adult children and preparing them for work. Workplaces with the necessary physical and organizational accommodations for persons with disabilities exist more in theory than in practice. Even as they age and develop infirmities themselves, many of these parents continue to provide care for their adult child. There are few community supports for these families.

Life course theory is therefore a particularly useful framework for understanding the family dynamics of medical conditions, rehabilitation, enablement, and participation in the lives of children with disabilities. It recognizes that children with disabilities interact with their parents and siblings to structure ongoing family relations (often called family functioning). Their life courses are linked; as the life of a child with a disability in the family affects the members of that family, so too the family affects the life of the child with a disability. This process is ongoing, since as the life of one person changes, other family members may have changed responsibilities or new opportunities that can have long-term impacts on the course of their lives.

Thus, for example, when a child's disability requires a mother to quit work and provide round-the-clock home care, fathers typically try to increase their earnings by working longer hours, securing better paying jobs, or undertaking multiple jobs. As the child gets older and is able to attend school, the mother may be able to return to work, at least on a part-time basis, and the father may return to holding only one job.

These changes depend on the income the mothers could earn by returning to work, the help and assistance they receive from other family members, and the parents' ability to access satisfactory medical and school care and enablements. The changing needs and abilities of children with disabilities thus alter the situations of others in their families.

As a result of these linked life course experiences, these family members are stressed, more often depressed, and less happy in their day-to-day lives. Yet at the same time, parents take satisfaction in their commitment to enabling their children with disabilities. They see themselves and their families meeting the challenges they face and coping well with the complexities of raising a child with a disability.

## The Study

It is my belief that information from informal and semi-structured interviews, unstructured observation, and representative population data together allows me to draw an original, realistic, and comprehensive picture of families raising children with disabilities. Here, I briefly describe how I approached the study of children's disabilities and the information and methods I used. Chapter 2 gives a complete description of the study methodology.

The World Health Organization's (WHO) International Classification of Functioning, Disability, and Health, and its 2007 adaptation to children, provide the rubric for conceptualizing children's disabilities. The most relevant elements of the WHO framework for this study include medical impairments (medical conditions that are potentially disabling), limitations in the ability to do everyday activities (walk, dress, eat, understand, communicate, learn, concentrate), and limitations in the ability to participate in social life and age-appropriate roles (play with peers, attend school, work, live independently). An important innovation in the WHO framework is its attention to the ways in which physical and social environments limit the ability to participate when a child, adolescent, or young adult has limitations in his or her ability to do daily tasks. While the term "rehabilitation" suggests that a person with a disability needs to be "fixed" to participate in life, "enablement" refers to helping persons overcome limitations in daily activities to allow full participation in daily life. Enablement includes rehabilitation (surgeries and drugs, therapies, prosthetics, and education supports), but it also goes beyond this to include improvements in the physical and social environment that remove barriers to participation.

I use twenty-four interviews with parents of children who receive occupational and vocational therapy at the Children's Rehabilitation Center. These interviews were organized in a conversational format to reduce the stress parents experience in discussing the positive and negative aspects of raising a child with a disability and to permit me to uncover new insights into causal connections. After studying this information there were still important unanswered questions. I then conducted my own interviews with six families of children with disabilities to fill in these gaps. I was also privileged to stay with one family whose son had severe cerebral palsy to supplement my own experiences with families raising children with disabilities.

Complementing this qualitative information, I use data that is representative of the entire population to measure how many families are raising children with disabilities, to investigate the extent to which some unfavorable family outcomes (such as divorce, required changes in patterns of work, income loss, and stress) are likely, and to estimate the extent to which families are able to adapt to and cope with the special challenges of raising children with disabilities. For this, I use the 2000 U.S. Census and seven surveys of the American population. Census 2000 included 157,000 children, age six and older, with disabilities, and the seven surveys in combination include 55,142 children with disabilities, including children of all ages. Together, the Census and surveys include information about children from birth to adolescence and from adolescence to the early years of adult life. They also include information about the lives of parents, brothers, sisters, and the family.

## An American Issue

The family costs of meeting the national mandate for the enablement of children with disabilities are seldom appreciated. Families of children with disabilities see family strengths and some advantages in their situations. This book shows that mothers, fathers, brothers, and sisters make many sacrifices when their family includes a child with a disability. By identifying the most difficult challenges they face, this study will show the compelling national need to support these families. Greater social and public supports for parents raising children with disabilities are essential to family well-being.

I hope that families of children with disabilities will find this book helpful. I aim to show that many of the costs, adaptations, and perplexities associated with having a child with a disability happen to parents whose children have mild and serious disabilities, and not just to families whose children have severe disabilities. Families also will see that the challenges and struggles of raising children with disabilities are due in large part to the huge societal expectations placed on the parents and the poor institutional arrangements that are available to help them. I also hope that professionals working with children with disabilities and their families will bring to their work a better under-standing of the overall challenges that families—particularly parents—face. Finally, I trust that readers of this book will be better able to recognize the contributions to American life made by families of children with disabilities and will be inspired to help reduce the family consequences of raising children with disabilities in the United States.

# = Chapter 2 =

## Methods to Study
## Family Consequences of
## Children's Disabilities[1]

I N CHAPTER 1, I briefly explained how I conceptualize children's disabilities and indicated the types of information I use. Readers less interested in the methodological aspects of this study can simply go to chapter 3. Readers who are not interested in statistical details can also ignore textual reports of odds ratios (OR) and levels of statistical significance ($p < .05$), as well as other material presented in brackets. If readers ignore these statistical and methodological details, the material in the rest of the book is still accessible. I hope that potential readers of this book are not put off by the inclusion in the text of these additional methodological and statistical details; the text is written to be accessible to all audiences—parents; medical and educational specialists; social workers; nurses who work with families in the community; other community health care experts; policymakers at the local, state, and national levels; and journalists. Just skip ahead to chapter 3 if you do not wish to know more about the science behind these details.

The methodologies I used are detailed in this chapter to provide information for readers who want to independently assess the scientific quality of the study. Underlying this summary information are very complex issues that need to be explained in detail. This chapter provides a full description of the conceptual framework for studying children's disabilities. It also gives considerable detail on the sources of information used in the study and the methodologies for collecting that information, discusses the accuracy of the information, and indicates the weaknesses and strengths of each source of information while highlighting how the different sources complement each other.

### Framework for the Study of Disability

I use the World Health Organization (WHO) framework for the classification of disability among children. In an unprecedented multiyear effort, the WHO brought together worldwide panels of health professionals and other disability experts, the public, and government and health agencies to come up with a way to classify and analyze disabilities for persons of all ages (Simeonsson et al. 2000). The WHO framework is a modification and extension of several prior frameworks that researchers used for the study of disability, with the potential for universal acceptance.

The WHO framework, known as the International Classification of Functioning, Disability, and Health (ICF) model, describes a person's health and well-being in terms of four components: body structures, body functions, activities, and participation (WHO 2001). Disabilities in activities and limitations in participation are the aspects of disability most readily measured in population surveys. The WHO framework emphasizes the idea that disability results from the interaction of medical conditions, ability in activities, and social environments.[2] Within the WHO-ICF framework, body functions are the physiological functions of body systems, including motor, sensory, and psychological systems, such as concentrating, remembering, and thinking. Problems with body structures typically can be determined only through careful medical examination and a variety of diagnostic tests and data are available to researchers only through medical records. These tests typically are not performed unless a medical condition is identified (except for cases of heritable body function variations that family history suggests should be investigated).

Medical doctors, mental health experts, and other health specialists measure disabilities in body functions as medical impairments or medical conditions, and these are noted in medical records. It is not, in practical terms, possible to use direct physician reports matched to survey information on children with disabilities. (In one attempt to use physician forms on infant health data, I found that far too few health professionals completed the forms, and in many cases the records were incomplete and the quality of data appeared to be poor.)

In population surveys, one way to identify medical impairments is to ask family respondents if a doctor or other specialist has told them that their child has a medical condition. Parents can be asked to respond to a checklist of common medical conditions. Some population surveys ask about medical impairments. I use this information as an independent variable in the models estimated in order to separate the influence of medical conditions from the impact of functional and participation disabilities on families.

The activities that children with disabilities can or cannot do are the most salient for families' daily lives (Hogan and Msall 2007). Activities refer to daily tasks such as communicating, walking, carrying things, eating, dressing, toileting, bathing, and learning. Survey respondents typically are asked a series of questions about their children's activity limitations in mobility (for example, walking short distances or getting in and out of a chair) and self-care (for example, the ability to bathe or shower or independently handle toileting, dressing, and silverware), as well as sensory and communication limitations (seeing, hearing, speaking) and learning limitations. Each of the population surveys used in this book includes some questions that measure disabilities in activities. This makes it possible to do a comprehensive study of the family consequences of children's disabilities, drawing on the strengths of each of the population surveys.

Many diagnosed medical conditions are associated with limitations in the ability to learn (either in relation to other children or as diagnosed by a professional). Children who have profound limitations in sight, hearing, or the ability to speak often are limited in their ability to learn at the same pace as other children. In this study, I consider children who have learning difficulties that are associated with physical or sensory limitations. I also include children who have been diagnosed with intellectual disability, Down syndrome, or developmental disabilities (such as autism, cerebral palsy, or muscular dystrophy). The Individuals with Disabilities Education Act (IDEA) of 1997 recognizes other types of learning limitations that do not arise from physical problems with mobility, self-care, communication, or obvious physical disability and are not due to poverty or social disadvantage (Lyon 1996). The U.S. Department of Education labels these medically undiagnosed learning limitations as "learning disabilities." The definition I use is broader— children with all types of disability in learning, regardless of cause, are included as learning disabled.

Mental health problems such as depression, bipolar disorder, schizophrenia, and eating disorders are only roughly measured in population surveys. Surveys typically have general indicators of mental health issues, but these are expressed in terms of how they limit activities of daily living and participation. Thus, for example, a survey might ask whether a limitation in activities—in this case the ability to learn—is due to a "delay or problem in emotional or behavioral development" or a "delay or problem in mental development."

Disabilities in participation are another aspect of the WHO framework. Participation means involvement in community life. Depending on age, this can mean playing with peers; maintaining relationships with family; attending school; holding a job; and being involved in religious, civic, and social groups. Population surveys can be quite good at measuring participation, but many surveys, especially those designed to collect health and disability information, have information only on school enrollment and special education. Other population surveys focus on social and economic behaviors of adolescents and young adults and collect more information on participation, but have less detailed information about young people's disabilities.

The extent to which disabilities in activities limit participation is one indicator of the severity of disabilities. Another common indicator of the seriousness of disabilities in surveys is whether activities require assistance. Population surveys also sometimes measure the seriousness of activity limitations by asking whether the limitation matters "a little" or "a lot." Each of these strategies is employed in one or more of the population surveys used in this study. One of the challenges of this study, then, is these variations in the measurement of medical impairments and disabilities and limitations in activity and participation. I have tried to make the measurement across surveys as comparable as possible and to be clear about the advantages and limitations of each population survey.

The ICF model recognizes that disabilities in activities cause "handicaps" in participation when there are unfavorable physical and social environments. Overall, however, it points to broader organizational and institutional environments as decisive in the extent to which disabilities in activities limit participation. These environmental factors include the organization of health, education, and employment services; legal protections; physical barriers; and discriminatory practices. I am unable to look at health care and educational institutions with the population data. Cultural and resource barriers to services help explain why some children are more likely than others to have activity disabilities that lead to limitations in participation. Of course, children themselves affect the kind of school programs they are offered, and this may change over time. This is not captured in the survey data but was addressed in the interviews.

## Enablement

"Rehabilitation" is the word commonly used to describe the help that children who are limited in their abilities to do everyday tasks receive in order to participate more fully in society. Rehabilitation typically locates the cause of a disability in individual persons, with the goal of using surgery, medical devices, and special equipment to allow the person to function in the same way as someone without disabilities.

However, "enablement" is a better term to describe how families try to empower their children who have disabilities. Enablement includes modifying the physical, family, and social environments to fit with the particular abilities of children who would otherwise be limited in activities or participation. This distinction is important to parents—they work with children to improve their abilities to be self-reliant in daily activities, but at the same time they constantly seek changes in children's environments that improve children's abilities to participate. To parents, enablement means helping children with disabilities reach their full potential.

Population surveys do better at measuring rehabilitation than enablement. The interviews with mothers at the Children's Rehabilitation Center give insights into enablement efforts by parents and families. One of the most important ways in which parents promote an enabling environment is through advocating for their children in school. This is a recurrent theme in interviews with parents.

I extend the WHO model of disability to include the consequences of a child's disability for mothers, fathers, brothers and sisters, and entire families. I see these family consequences as products of the children's disabilities in activities, the costs of rehabilitation and enablement, and disabilities in participation.

## Strategies for the Measurement of Child Disability

The survey definition of disabilities among older persons follows well established and accepted procedures. There is not yet scientific agreement on how to use population surveys to measure children's disabilities. The definition of disability among children is complicated by variations in classifications of disability across institutions, funding mechanisms, and the discipline of the researchers (Hogan, Park, and Holder 2004) and because the term itself is so broad and subjective. The conditions that limit a child's ability to perform everyday tasks and participate in age-appropriate roles are often contested by both parents and medical professionals; while parents may have an "official" diagnosis by a health specialist, mental health professional, or a special education teacher, they may disagree with those providing the diagnosis. Some parents may regard a medical condition as severely limiting but the health professional may not, leading to different expectations about social participation. The physical and social environments in which children live also shape whether a medical impairment becomes a handicap. Societal perceptions of a child as being "different" or "disabled" affect the children's perception of limitations in activities and their families' perceptions, as well.

### Shortcomings of Medical Diagnosis

The problems of using only a diagnosis of a medical condition to measure child disability are illustrated by the situations of children with cerebral palsy. Sometimes a child is diagnosed as having cerebral palsy at birth or shortly after. In other cases, parents may notice their child is not developing as quickly or in the same way as other children and may seek a medical opinion that results in the diagnosis of cerebral palsy at age two; however, some children are not diagnosed until much later. Many children with cerebral palsy have only minor limitations in their ability to walk, skip, climb stairs, or run. Other children may be able to perform these motor functions with surgery, rehabilitation, or leg braces. In yet other cases, children with cerebral palsy are in wheelchairs. Whether in a wheelchair or physically mobile, some children with cerebral palsy have limitations in small motor skills (dressing, toileting, or eating), while others do not. They may have no limitations in learning, or they may be profoundly limited in their ability to learn.

All of these children have been diagnosed with cerebral palsy, but their specific abilities and disabilities mean that their lives are very different. A family whose child has cerebral palsy but who has no limitations in self-care and learning is affected by this diagnosis much differently than a family whose child with cerebral palsy is in a wheelchair, needs help with self-care because of limited small motor skills, and has cognitive limitations in learning. I focus on limitations in children's abilities to do activities of daily living and examine the impact of activity limitations on their ability to participate in play, school, and work. Capturing the severity of activity disabilities in survey research sometimes depends on having information about the extent to which they limit age-appropriate social roles; in other cases, the degree to which disabilities in activities are serious is measured by whether equipment or personal assistance is needed to perform certain tasks. When possible, I also take into account the medical conditions of the children as reported by the parents, but I concentrate on information on daily activities and participation since these aspects often have the greatest import for families.

## Accuracy of Parents' Reports

While measuring disability based solely on medical diagnosis is imperfect, questions to identify children's disabilities in activities and participation are straightforward. Parents with different levels of education typically are equally able to answer questions about whether or not their children have difficulties (none, some, a lot) or need assistance in such activities as bathing or showering, dressing, eating, getting in or out of bed or chairs, using the toilet, getting around inside the home, or speaking well enough to communicate their needs to family members. Questions about learning disabilities in surveys do not rely on parents' assessments of capacity to learn—instead parents are asked whether they have been told their child has disabilities in learning. However, bias can arise in the reporting of learning disabilities because diagnosis is less likely in poorly resourced schools. Immigrant parents from Latin America less often report their children as having learning disabilities, in part because difficulties in learning may be confounded with children's English language skills. By focusing on activity limitations and ability to participate in age-appropriate activities, I use the survey data that is least subject to reporting bias (Hogan and Msall 2007).

Survey data on medical conditions, services, and treatments can be biased, and thus using such data is a poor way to identify children with disabilities. Poor parents are less likely to have access to medical specialists who can provide sophisticated diagnoses. Less educated parents are less able to accurately remember and report complex diagnoses. Families with more economic resources (including medical insurance) are quicker to bring their children to health professionals when they exhibit some delay in development or health problem. Better educated parents are also more likely to understand and accurately remember the medical conditions of their children, especially when the nature of the disability is complex and involves many medical conditions.

Since they are involved in taking children to therapies or administering medications or treatments at home, parents are reasonably accurate in reporting the types of medications or services their children receive. However, children from poor families are less likely to get needed medical and educational services. If I identified children who have disabilities using information on medical conditions or the receipt of medications or services, this study would be seriously biased against the inclusion of families with fewer socioeconomic resources; it is these families for whom the consequences of a child's disabilities may be greatest.

A frequent objection to using parent reports of disability in activities is that they are not as good as the "gold standard" set by health or education professionals. While this is true for medical conditions, it is not relevant for activity limitations. In fact, professionals rely on parents' reports to determine if children are able to bathe themselves, eat with silverware, walk a city block, or communicate with their families. Parent reports of activity limitations in a carefully designed survey are at least as accurate as parent reports on a medical intake form or in an interview with a physician who is pressed for time. I believe that parents' responses to carefully designed surveys administered by trained interviewers are the gold standard for information about children's limitations in activities and participation in school or work.

## Sources of Information

In this book, I use a combination of population surveys that are available to researchers (quantitative data) and semi-structured interviews with mothers of children with disabilities that were done for this study (qualitative data). It is useful to combine these two types of information for several reasons. In many ways, the semi-structured interviews provide the most powerful picture of the impact of having a child with disability, since as mothers they have the daily experience of life with a disabled child. Their "job," as in most other families, is to maintain the well-being of their families, monitoring how things are going with each member. (This is not to say that fathers cannot do this, just that in the United States they typically do this less than mothers.) These mothers struggle not only with caring and advocating for their children with disabilities but also with schedules, finances, and homemaking for the entire family.

These interviews provide illustrative data that help interpret the broader statistical studies that I use. These semi-structured interviews are intended to be illustrative; they are not used in an attempt to conduct a full-fledged ethnographic study. Such informal qualitative work has been done in many other studies of children with disabilities and their families, but these studies have lacked representative population coverage. The contribution of my study is to represent the entire population of children with disabilities and their families with survey information and then to use focused interviews to interpret and inform the population results. The interviews also provide information on family contact with health care agencies and social institutions that the survey data do not.

### Interviews

Interviews were conducted with twenty-four mothers who are primary caregivers of children with disabilities receiving physical and/or occupational therapies at the Children's Rehabilitation Center. This center is affiliated with a hospital located in a large city in New England. These mothers have a child or children with disability who are two or more years old. The children have a physical condition that limits their activities and results from a medical impairment, such as cerebral palsy, spina bifida, or muscular dystrophy. Face-to-face semi-structured interviews were carried out while the mothers waited during their children's therapy sessions. This was an ideal place and time to do these interviews, as the mothers had time and often were bored, and the interviews gave them the chance to talk about their experiences with a special-needs child. This research was approved by the Brown University Institutional Review Board and by the hospital in which the Children's Rehabilitation Center is housed.

Semi-structured interviews have particular topics to cover, but the questions and responses are informal and conversational. The interview topics were selected to help interpret the findings from the statistical analysis of the population information. The topics included social support, marital and family relationships, mother's and father's work and home roles, economic impacts, brothers and sisters, and the decision to have additional children. The interview session concluded by asking the mothers to complete a brief, structured questionnaire. The questionnaire gathered information on family demographics, family financial situation, and participation in special programs sometimes available for children with disabilities. The interviews were audio recorded and then transcribed into text files. Each interview lasted an average of one hour.

Mothers were assured that their names and their children's names would not be used and that their children's right to medical care confidentiality would be protected. They were also fully informed about the purpose of the study. This allowed them to decide whether they wished to be contacted and participate, particularly as the topics covered in the interviews dealt with potentially sensitive issues that they might have found uncomfortable or threatening. All references to clinics, hospitals, and names of mothers, fathers, siblings, and children in these interviews are pseudonyms.

Although I had permission to access medical records for children at the Children's Rehabilitation Center (with Health Insurance Portability and Accountability Act [HIPAA] approval), I chose not to use this information as a further guarantee of confidentiality for the families. In this study, when I describe the medical condition of a child in the Children's Rehabilitation Center, the information comes from the parent interview and not from medical records. Parent statements of children's medical impairments may sometimes be inaccurate, but they reflect the information that parents use in making decisions about their children's treatments and potential.

In addition, I got information from a number of families outside of the Children's Rehabilitation Center. Their children have other sorts of disabilities (such as autism, cerebral palsy with sensory and communication disorders, Down syndrome, and Rett syndrome). I also talked to two families whose children with disabilities had died before the initial interview.

## Surveys

No single population survey provides the information I needed for this study. Instead, I use information from a census and seven nationally representative population surveys that together capture the full range of children's disabilities and their family consequences. I use surveys that (1) are representative of the population of American children, (2) identify children with disabilities in activities, (3) include sufficient numbers of children with disabilities to estimate statistical models, and

(4) include some information about families (such as ethnicity, family structure, education of parent[s], and income or poverty status). I used the most recent surveys that were available at the time of the data analysis. In analyzing information on children's disabilities from the census and surveys, I distinguish, when possible, between disabilities in self-care (such as bathing, dressing, eating, toileting), mobility (such as walking short distances, getting in and out of chairs), senses (hearing and seeing) and communication (ability to speak), cognitive deficits, and mental and behavioral health.

The Census 2000 (Ruggles et al. 2010b) was the first U.S. census to include questions about disabilities in activities for children ages five to fifteen. A 6 percent sample of household and person records is available for research use and includes 157,000 children with disabilities in physical mobility, self-care, eyesight and hearing, and cognitive capacity (concentrating, learning, and remembering).

The census provides detailed social and economic information for households and for individual persons who are members of families, permitting me to identify children with disabilities, their family environments, and the social and economic situations of parents and other family members.

Matched data are from two population surveys: the National Survey of Family Growth (NSFG)[3] and the National Health Interview Survey (NHIS).[4] A special data set was created for this study to examine the impact that children with disabilities who are ages three to fourteen have on family life. Combining marriage and fertility information collected in the 1995 NSFG with information on children's disabilities from the 1993 NHIS, this data set illustrates how the disability status of children affects mothers' family lives. This was the last time the NSFG and NHIS used the same sampling frame so that there was an overlap of persons in the two surveys. This matched data set includes some 10,000 pairs of women and children; 650 children have a disability in participation in school, and for 62 of these children, the disability severely limits participation.

The NHIS provides the major source of information with which to monitor the health of the American population. The NHIS collects information on the health, health status, and participation disability of persons of all ages. By combining the NHIS panels for seven years from 1997 to 2003, I identified 8,276 children ages five to seventeen for whom there was detailed information about disabilities. (I did not extend the time series beyond 2003, as the 2004 data had problems with a severe over-reporting of the number of children with cerebral palsy.) The NHIS provides information to study the effects of a child's disability on the health and health care of other family members.

The National Health Interview Survey on Disability (NHISD)[5] was the first national survey (1994 and 1995) focused specifically on chronic health conditions and disabilities in the American population. A 1995 followback survey included a supplement that asked parents about children with special health care needs. The NHISD collected unusually detailed information on the health and disability status of children (medical conditions, activity limitations, and disabilities in participation), including a detailed inventory of medical services and equipment and educational resources for children's rehabilitation and enablement. The NHISD asked whether the health condition and disability of the child caused labor force changes, financial loss, and sleep deprivation for family members. (Since I selected NHISD children who had activity limitations, these questions on impact relate to the effects of disability rather than medical conditions per se.) The NHISD sample for this study included 3,500 children ages five to seventeen with activity disabilities. This survey is the last date for which this detailed information is available; a new NHISD is now under way. The NHISD remains the best tool for the measurement of the number of children with disabilities.

The National Survey of Children with Special Health Care Needs (CSHCN)[6] interviewed, by telephone, the families of 215,000 children under the age of eighteen in 2002 and 2003. The CSHCN classified children as having special health care needs if they regularly need or use medicine prescribed by a doctor; need or use more medical care, mental health, or educational services than is usual for most children; are limited or prevented in their ability to do things; require or receive special therapy; or require or receive special treatment for an emotional, developmental, or behavioral problem (Newacheck et al. 1998; Van Dyck et al. 2002). The study identified 39,000 children with special health care needs, of whom 36,568 had disabilities. With the CSHCN, I am able to compare the effects of disabilities on family life with the experience of families of children who have chronic health conditions but are not disabled. The CSHCN collected information about children's medical care, health insurance, access to needed services, and coordination of care (Van Dyck et al. 2002). This survey gives the best information for my study of the complex struggles families face in getting appropriate medical care for their children with disabilities and parents' struggles with the health care system. It also asked parents their perceptions of the impact of their children's specific medical conditions, disabilities, and service needs on the family.

The National Survey of Children's Health (NSCH)[7] included a national sample of 102,000 children under the age of eighteen, of whom 3,833 had disabilities in participation. (The NSCH did not collect the information necessary to identify specific types of children's disabilities in activities.) In 2003 and 2004, it collected a variety of information about children's physical, emotional, and behavioral health; parental health; family stress; parental coping behaviors; family activities; and parental concerns. I use the NSCH to look at the complex challenges families face in raising children with disabilities in participation and the impacts of children's disabilities on maternal stress and coping behaviors.

The National Longitudinal Survey of Youth (NLSY)[8] followed 9,000 children, most of whom were twelve to sixteen years old in 1997, for eight years until they were ages twenty through twenty-four in 2005. After removing cases for missing data on the disability measure and allowing for parents' non-response in 1997, the effective sample size was 7,590, of whom 789 had mild disabilities and 228 had serious disabilities (determined by parent reports that the disability existed and mattered "a little" or "a lot"). The data from the NLSY allows me to investigate differences between children with and without disabilities in adolescent social behaviors and interactions with peers and parents, high school academic performance, college plans and attendance, and employment.

The NLSY followed an actual cohort of children over an extended period for their life course, with information provided by the adolescents themselves. Because of this, the NLSY excludes adolescents with cognitive disabilities that are serious enough to prevent them from being interviewed. It is therefore important to keep in mind that children with disabilities in the NLSY do not have the extensive cognitive disabilities of some children included in the other population surveys. Even so, the effects of disability on adolescent behaviors and achievements are considerable.

An earlier study, the National Longitudinal Transition Study of Special Education Students (NLTS)[9] of 1985, surveyed families of children ages thirteen to twenty-one who were enrolled in special education programs and followed them for five years until they were eighteen to twenty-six years old. Information for this study was collected from parents and primary caregivers. This study includes 2,065 students who participated in both the initial and follow-up surveys. Children's specific disabilities were determined by the special education classification used by schools. To compare the NLTS sample with the population of school-age children who do not have disabilities, I used the National Education Longitudinal Survey (NELS). The NLTS-NELS data complement the NLSY by allowing me to follow how cohorts of young persons with serious disabilities (including those who cannot participate in an interview) transition into adulthood—for example, whether they are able to become residentially independent, take on some form of employment, or form their own families.

## Number of Children with Disabilities

How many children in the United States have disabilities in activities? Because of developmental delays at younger ages, the measurement of

Table 2.1    Type of Disability in Activities, Children Age Five to Seventeen

| | Population with Disability | Rate per 1000 | | |
|---|---|---|---|---|
| Activity Limitation | | Total Disability | Mild Disability | Serious Disability |
| Mobility | 698,000 | 13.1 | 10.9 | 2.2 |
| Self-care | 506,000 | 9.5 | 4.4 | 5.1 |
| Sensory/communication | 2,946,000 | 55.3 | 28.3 | 27.0 |
| Learning/behavior | 5,823,000 | 109.3 | 34.3 | 71.4 |
| Any limitation | 6,537,000 | 122.7 | 41.9 | 80.8 |

Source: Author's tabulations of National Health Interview Survey on Disability rates (Centers for Disease Control and Prevention 1995) applied to 2008 U.S. Census population counts (Ruggles et al. 2010b).

children with disabilities is best done for children ages five and older. The best population estimates of children with disabilities who are ages five to seventeen can be obtained from the NHISD, since that survey has the most comprehensive battery of questions about medical conditions, activity limitations, and participation. Table 2.1 illustrates the rate of disability in activities per 1000 children. About 122.7 children per 1000 (6,537,000 children) have any activity disability. The rates of disabilities in mobility (13.1 per 1000, or 698,000 children) and self-care (9.5 per 1000, or 506,000 children) are relatively low. About 55.3 children per 1000 (2,946,000 children) have disabilities in their ability to see, hear, speak, or communicate; one-half of these sensory and communication disabilities are serious. The most commonly observed disabilities involve learning and learning-disruptive behaviors. The rate of learning and behavior disabilities is 109.3 per 1,000 children (5,823,000 children); about two-thirds of these cases are serious. Many children with disabilities in mobility, self-care, and sensory communication also have learning and behavior disabilities.

Most American children (91 percent) attend regular programs in schools and are able to engage in play activities outside of school (Hogan et al. 1997). Another 5.2 percent of children (2,770,000) attend regular schools but are limited in what they can do (for example, participate in physical education classes) or require some assistance (such as speech or language therapy, reading assistance, or wheelchair use). Other children (1.4 percent, or 746,000 children) attend school but either are enrolled in schools specializing in children with disabilities or attend regular schools that have segregated, separate programs for students with disabilities. A small number of children with disabilities (0.3 percent, or about 160,000 children) are not able to attend school at all because of their disabilities. Another 2 percent of children (1,060,000 children) are not enrolled in school (for example, children who have dropped out of high school). Of all children with disabilities in activities, roughly 57 percent are mainstreamed in regular schools. This is consistent with the principles of the Individuals with Disabilities Education Act that specify that American children with disabilities should attend, to the extent feasible, regular schools along with their peers.

Only 5 percent of children with disabilities in activities lack a medical diagnosis. Only 3 percent of children who are limited in their schooling have no diagnosed medical condition. While most children with disabilities have a medical impairment, not all children with medical conditions have disabilities. In fact, fewer than one in five children with chronic diseases, medical conditions that occur episodically, and asthma have serious disabilities in activities (Msall et al. 2003). This classification of medical impairments takes medical condition information recorded in the NHISD and codes it into the International Classification of Diseases, Ninth Revision.

Thirty-three percent of children with chronic conditions, including 25 percent of children with asthma, are somewhat limited in their school attendance. The medical conditions most often associated with serious disabilities in children are cognitive impairment (formerly designated as mental retardation); Down syndrome; autism spectrum disorders; cerebral palsy; vision, hearing, and communication disorders; injuries with effects lasting twelve months or longer; and problems with behavior and learning (such as anxiety, depression, and attention deficit–hyperactivity disorders). Only 7 percent of children with cognitive limitations and autism attend regular school, and of those, 79 percent are quite likely to need special education. About one-third of children with other seriously disabling medical conditions are limited in their schooling.

In recent years, there has been a great deal of attention focused on children with cognitive impairment (that is, mental retardation), intellectual disability, and developmental disabilities (Hogan, Msall, and Drew 2008). About 14 children per 1000 (1.4 percent of all children) ages five to seventeen have either limitations in intellectual ability (mental retardation) or developmental disabilities; one-half of the children with limitations in intellectual ability or developmental delays are cognitively impaired. Cerebral palsy remains a major factor in developmental disabilities (4 children per 1000 in the population). The increased prevalence of autism is also a major cause of developmental disabilities (measured in this population survey as 3 children per 1000 children in the population). Autism is now the medical condition associated with about one in five cases of children with intellectual limitations and developmental disabilities. While these rates appear low, the numbers of children involved are substantial—210,000 children with cerebral palsy, 160,000 with autism, and about 80,000 with Down syndrome. Of all children with cognitive impairment and developmental disabilities, more than 80 percent have one or more serious disabilities in activities. (Note that these are survey-based point prevalence estimates; they resemble estimates based on medical surveillance systems.)

## Family Situations Associated with Disability

Using information on activity limitations in the NHISD, I developed a summary measure of disability to capture the complexity (number of dimensions) and seriousness of the disabilities of children (Hogan et al. 1997). Children with mild disabilities are those who have one or more mild limitations in activities; 4.2 percent of American children ages five to seventeen have mild disabilities. Another 6.1 percent of children have one serious disability with any number of mild disabilities. Severe disabilities (that is, two or more serious limitations with any number of mild disabilities) characterize 2.1 percent of school-age children.

I estimated an ordered logistic regression that looked at the seriousness of children's disabilities using this summary measure (Hogan et al. 1997) based on relevant background and family factors. The ordered disability status outcomes are represented by the categories of severity of disability status (no limitation, mild limitation, one serious limitation, two or more serious limitations), focusing on limitations in activities. The model gives parameter estimates for the unique effects of various characteristics of children's families (Hogan et al. 1997).

Black children are just as likely as white children to have a disability, if not more serious disabilities, once their lower family resources are taken into account. Children of Hispanic origin have lower levels of disability in activities according to their parents; this is largely due to the selectivity of healthy children in the migrant population and the parents' belief that schools incorrectly diagnose their children with learning disabilities when in fact their poorer performance is a result of language difficulties. Children in one-parent families are 62 percent more likely than children in two-parent families to have limitations in everyday activities as well as disabilities that are more serious. Children living apart from their parents are twice as likely to have higher levels of disability as children living with two parents. Children living with their mothers and another adult (a grandparent or a mother's sexual partner) have disability statuses similar to those of children from two-parent families. Children in families in which the parents have less than a college education have slightly higher levels of disability. Children whose families live in poverty are 40 percent more likely to have a disability compared to children whose families do not live in poverty, and, if they have a disability, to have one that is more limiting.

These results are descriptive; no statistical analysis can establish causation. It is not possible, for example, to tell whether the greater odds of disability among poor children are a result of family poverty. It may be that families with few resources are more likely to have children with potentially disabling medical conditions due to such factors as insufficient prenatal care or that poor families are less able to mobilize the treatments that would prevent medical conditions from becoming disabling. It is possible, too, that having a child with a disability could lead to having lower parental earnings because of the need to spend more time with the child or could more likely lead to divorce, resulting in more one-parent households in which a child has a disability. Using a number of strategies, this book aims to disentangle the directions of the relationships between family situations and children's disabilities.

I rely heavily on parents' education as a measure of family resource situations since it is typically established before children are born. Parents' reports about family outcomes that have resulted from their children's disabilities are especially helpful in establishing the family consequences of children's disabilities. The interpretations of the survey data based on the interviews with mothers at the Children's Rehabilitation Center are also helpful. Finally, by examining a broad range of child and family behaviors at different points over the linked life courses of children with disabilities and their parents and siblings, it is clear that there are pervasive and large consequences for families raising children with disabilities.

## Statistical Analysis

The results of these analyses are presented in a table and simple figures throughout this book. However, I recognize that it is essential that these relationships of family situations with disability and of children's disability with a multiplicity of family consequences take into account a variety of confounding factors. As indicated in the text, I did conduct such analyses using models (typically logistic regression models); I report whether the relationship described persists net of a variety of other variables. Where it seems useful, I also show relevant odds ratios that describe the family consequences of children's disabilities, controlling for other variables.

We now turn to an examination of the family consequences of raising children with disabilities.

# = Chapter 3 =

## Supporting, Growing, and Dissolving the Family[1]

**M**ANY PARENTS live together when a child with a disability is born; many other parents do not live together when a child is born or at the time the child is diagnosed as having a disability. Parents are more likely to be married or living together in a stable relationship if both of them grew up in a two-parent family, have at least a high school education, are in their mid-twenties or older, and are white. Couples with these same traits are more likely to stay together. However, these parental traits have little impact on whether a child has a disability at birth, and the marital status of parents when a child is born is unlikely to be affected by knowledge of the infant's disability status before birth.

As children age beyond infancy, however, the challenges of raising a child with a disability begin to accumulate: gender roles may become more traditional, with mothers being responsible for caregiving and fathers becoming the primary breadwinners. Mothers and fathers may disagree on medical treatments and behavioral interventions, and many families have insufficient income to meet their needs. These challenges can lead to marital conflict, cause parents to recognize that their child is more difficult to raise, or even lower parents' satisfaction with family life (see chapter 4). These factors all increase the chances that the parents will separate or divorce.

For parents of a child with a disability, these challenges and the family's coping strategies all contribute to whether the parents will remain married. Fathers of children with disabilities who are wholly or largely absent from their children's lives place additional financial and caregiving burdens on the mothers of their children. Parents who remain together face decisions about whether to have additional children. While all married couples make decisions about remaining together or separating and about how many children to have, these considerations are critical for parents raising a child with a disability, as having a child with a disability makes everything more complicated.

## Marriage and Divorce

Parents often are shocked and depressed when they find out that their child has a disability. When interviewed at the Children's Rehabilitation Center, Laura said that she became very depressed after the birth of her son Anthony when she learned that he had cerebral palsy:

> I remember it like it was yesterday . . . very hard and the depression really started to affect my life. I started to not love myself, I didn't take care of myself, I wouldn't eat, I would sleep all the time, I wouldn't fix myself up, it didn't matter what day it was but I started to notice that it was causing my daughters to suffer to see me like this. Sad, crying, and I think the older one suffered a lot to see me like that, and I struggle a lot with that. There are days that I say I can't take this anymore, I get frustrated.

Robert, whose daughter Erin has mild cerebral palsy, was present when his wife Marilyn was interviewed and noted that the greatest stress can be on the mother of a disabled child:

> Well, the beginning, it's very emotional. Psychologically. Because . . . it hurts your wife. Like she got very depressed [when their child's disability was diagnosed and they became aware of the medical care needs]. And even me, because you ask why do those things happen. But [eventually] it made us stronger.

The stress associated with learning their child has a disability is implicated in parents' experiences of separation or divorce. According to the National Survey of Children's Health (based on children younger than twelve months), 76 percent of children with disabilities live with two parents at birth, compared to 83 percent of children who do not have disabilities. (This difference at birth is partly due to the fact that more unmarried mothers access prenatal care later in pregnancy and are thus more likely to have babies who are premature or have low birth weight, factors that increase the likelihood of disability in an infant.)

Parents of children with disabilities who are together at birth often end their relationship soon after the birth of a child with a disability—30 percent of parents do so by the time the child is three years old (see figure 3.1). The differential in rate of divorce is less after the child reaches three years of age, but by then the differences are well established. By age ten, just over one-half of parents who were together at the time a child with a disability was born remain together, compared to three-quarters of parents raising a child without a disability.

The rate of divorce also can be calculated from the matched data of the National Survey of Family Growth and the National Health Inter-

**Figure 3.1    Parents' Relationships Remaining Intact During the First Ten Years After Birth, by Disability Status of the Child**

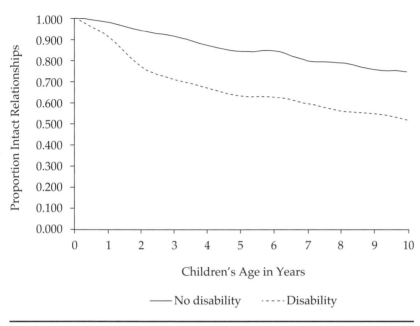

Children's Age in Years

———— No disability    · · · · · Disability

*Source:* Author's calculations of data from the National Survey of Children's Health (U.S. Department of Health and Human Services 2003).
*Note:* Parents' relationships include both marriage and cohabitation. This calculation is an approximation based on the proportion of parents who are still together at each year of the child's age and cumulating the implied probability that parents remain married from one year to the next, from birth to age ten. This is what demographers refer to as a synthetic cohort method. Using this procedure, it was not possible to control for other factors associated with parents' divorce.

view Survey. These data allow me to calculate true cohort rates of a marriage ending as well as estimate the divorce rate of parents who have children with severe disabilities. Compared to the data from the National Survey of Children's Health, however, the sample size is small and not as current. (Using a discrete-time event history model, rates of divorce were calculated by taking into account mothers' race and ethnicity, age at marriage, and education; the number and age of children; immigrant status; and rural residence.) Compared to couples whose child does not have a disability, the rate of divorce is more likely for parents of children with mild disabilities (odds ratio [OR] = 1.39, $p < .05$) and even more likely when the child has a severe disability (OR = 2.29, $p < .05$).

Clearly, mothers and fathers who are together at the birth of their child are more likely, compared to other parents, to separate or divorce if their child is disabled. This difference is concentrated in the first three years after birth. As a result, mothers of children with disabilities more often become single parents, with the attendant problems of lower family income as well as the need to assume sole responsibility for a child with special and sometimes extraordinary needs.

The interviews at the Children's Rehabilitation Center show that even for parents who are still married, having a child with a disability puts parents at greater risk of a divorce. Erin, who is eight, has a mild case of cerebral palsy, but her initial diagnosis was not promising. Her mother Marilyn believes that if she and her husband Robert had not been as close as they were before Erin was born, they probably would have split up:

> I mean, I have to be very honest, before having Erin, Robert and I were the envy of almost everyone we know. They were like, "You guys are like soulmates. You were put on the earth. It was absolutely inevitable that you two would meet because you're so compatible." And then the stresses of raising and getting a diagnosis and having a heart condition, and being up in the OR for the eye surgery. And me thinking I was home and nobody could do it as well as I can do it, I think it put a lot of stress on our relationship.

Ricky, age six, has developmental delays and limitations to his fine motor skills. His mother Debra believes it is unusual that she and Richard are still together:

> I have a friend that her husband was a policeman and she has a daughter with a disability. And Rich is a state trooper and we have Ricky with a disability. And she said, "Do you know the rate of divorce for people that are just married to policemen?" It's supposed to be really high. And the divorce rate of having children with special needs is really high. I'm like . . . it kind of makes you think, it's like, "Wow, we're doing alright, then, because if you had that profession and a child with a disability and you're still together."

## Changes in Employment When a Child Has a Disability

When a new child is born, all parents must decide whether the mother will be a stay-at-home caregiver and, if so, for how long. Some mothers who have worked outside the home decide to return to work within weeks of birth, while other mothers wait six months or a year to do so. The majority of women, however, return to work by their child's first birthday (unless they have other preschool-age children who need care) or, at the latest, by the time their child enters school. Typically, when a mother works outside the home, her child is in the care of other family members, informal child care, or a child care center. For many parents, both the mother and father need to work to pay for family necessities, especially housing. Recent changes in the welfare policies of the United States require single mothers with children to work after a brief period of income support. In addition to job earnings, many mothers want to return to work for the satisfaction they get from working and to make sure career progress is not delayed. When parents have a disabled child, however, all of these issues become more complicated, and their decisions about child care and employment are quite different.

The interviews with parents at the Children's Rehabilitation Center give insights into the employment decisions of parents of children with disabilities and how these can change. Married mothers and fathers sometimes share work and care of their disabled child. Robert, whose daughter Erin has cerebral palsy but is doing quite well in regular school, describes this division of labor:

> [We had] a number of [work] transitions. Marilyn has worked part-time, I've worked full-time. Then she worked full-time, and I didn't work for a while. And I went back full-time, and she went back full-time.

However, the family experienced considerable financial stress until both parents were working full-time and Erin was on support from the Katie Beckett program, a state government program that pays for the specialized food, diapers, equipment, and other supplies and services that a child with disabilities needs to remain at home and would get in a residential care facility. Similar programs exist in most states, although the name of the program varies across states.

Tara, whose daughter has cerebral palsy, was formerly a teacher, but now she no longer works. She describes the changing family decisions about child care and work:

> I had taken a leave after Sadie was born. . . . I would have had to go back after like five weeks, and I just wasn't ready, so I took that year off, and then, by the end of the second year . . . I just kind of, like, knew [something was wrong]. . . . So I took a second year of leave, and by that second year, that's when we figured out there was something wrong. And we

started with all these, like, many, many appointments, like I will just say, like, our whole life was, like, going to Sadie's appointments. And it just became obvious to me that there was, like, who would do this, like, if I went back to work and she was in daycare?

Even when mothers of children with disabilities do return to work, they are more likely than other mothers to stop working so they can provide full-time care. Carol has two daughters with disabilities. One of them, Katie, can only attend school three half-days per week. Carol relates:

First I was a schoolteacher, but then I became a school administrator because it was actually a part-time administrative position. . . . Eventually I stopped working. Although I enjoyed working, the girls' medical needs are just so great that you go to one appointment, it stems three other appointments. . . . We're usually either in the hospital two days a week or at a doctor's appointment. . . . My husband was doing very well at his job, I was doing well at my job [laughs], but we had to really decide. My career, I can hop in and out of, luckily.

Life history information in the matched National Survey of Family Growth and the National Health Interview Survey shows that mothers of children with disabilities are less likely to return to the labor force within the first two years after their child is born, compared to mothers whose children do not have disabilities. What is important, however, is that even when their children have serious disabilities, most mothers eventually return to paid employment and work during a substantial portion of their children's lives. Information for children who were able to participate in the National Longitudinal Survey of Youth (that is, adolescents who are able to be interviewed and complete a self-administered, computer-assisted survey) shows that on average, by the time children are twelve years old, mothers are employed during 62 percent of children's lives if there is no disability versus 56 percent for children with moderate limitations. For children with serious disabilities, mothers have still been employed during more than one-half (53 percent) of their children's lives. While work delays are more likely after a child with a disability is born and subsequent interruptions in employment are more frequent, it is clear that many children with disabilities experience life in a home with a working mother.

Decisions about work and child care are more difficult for unmarried mothers who alone must help their children with disabilities navigate specialized care, supply home-based medical care, provide economically for the family, and nurture and care for other children. This is the situation of Alicia, discussed in chapter 1, who is a single mother who lives in a subsidized housing unit with her three sons, including Derek, who was brain-damaged in an accident when he was four. Although Alicia reports considerable help from family members, she feels she is not able to work because of Derek's needs. The family lives in poverty and sometimes lacks money to buy food.

The situation of Connie, whose son Eric has cerebral palsy with extreme mental retardation, is quite different from that of Alicia. Because she is a wealthy widow with health insurance for her family, Connie can employ a full-time nurse for Eric. Even so, Connie has decided not to work. Unmarried mothers with fewer financial resources may have more pressure to work for family economic needs and to obtain employer-provided health insurance.

Information from the 2000 Census shows the work patterns of mothers of children with different types of disabilities (see figure 3.2). Mothers of all school-age children with disabilities are less likely to be employed if their child has a more serious type of disability. While 28 percent of mothers of children without disabilities are unemployed or not in the paid labor force at any given time, 42 percent of mothers of children with self-care disabilities (OR = 0.51, $p < .001$) are not in the labor force or unemployed, as are 39 percent of mothers of children with both sensory-physical and learning disabilities (OR = 0.87, $p < .001$).

Thus, mothers of disabled children are less likely to work for pay at any point in time. Being out of the workforce is likely due in part to the greater difficulties that these mothers have in balancing time-consuming disability treatments, services, and special home care responsibilities. Another issue is the difficulty of finding suitable and affordable child care for a special-needs child (Brandon 2000). Indeed, the lower rate of employment for single mothers of children with disabilities is as large as the lower rate of employment among mothers who themselves have a disability. As a result, single mothers of children with disabilities have a higher likelihood of becoming welfare dependent and experience greater difficulty in leaving welfare for employment (Brandon and Hogan 2004; Brandon, Hofferth, and Hogan 2008). Single mothers generally are less likely to have access to health insurance through their jobs than are fathers, and fear of losing public health insurance coverage is another reason single mothers of children with disabilities do not become employed (Guendelman, Wyn, and Tsai 2000).

Mary is a single mother who was interviewed at the Children's Rehabilitation Center. She manages to work full-time while getting the care her son Nathan needs. She does this through a flexible work schedule:

I took every Monday off. I worked on Saturday to make up for the Monday. So I didn't lose any pay or any time. But yeah, my company was very

**Figure 3.2   Mothers' Employment Patterns by Disability Status of the Child, Children Ages Five to Seventeen**

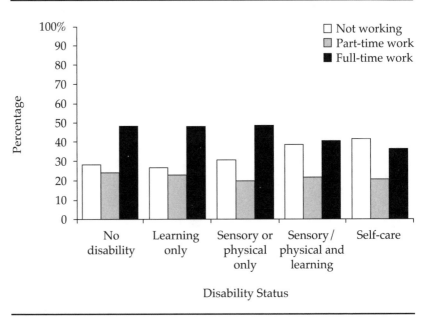

Source: Author's calculations of data from Census 2000, 6 percent sample (Ruggles et al. 2010b).
Note: Includes all mothers. "Not working" includes the unemployed and women not in the labor force.

accommodating. I would leave Sunday night with him [to travel to a medical center three hours away], we'd stay over. We'd get his treatment on Monday and then we drive back Monday night.

Figure 3.3 shows how child disability affects maternal employment for women of different marital statuses and education levels, compared to similar mothers raising children without disabilities through adjusted employment rates. Thus, for example, among unmarried mothers with less than a high school education, child disability is associated with a 20 percent lower rate of employment compared to similarly educated single mothers whose children do not have disabilities. Among unmarried mothers with a high school diploma, child disability is associated with a 24 percent lower rate of employment compared to unmarried mothers with a high school diploma who do not have a child with a disability. Among married mothers with less than a high school diploma who have a child with a disability, the rate of employment is

**Figure 3.3    Adjusted Difference Between Parents' Employment Rate if They Have a Child Age Five to Seventeen with a Disability Versus if They Do Not, by Parents' Level of Education and Marital Status**

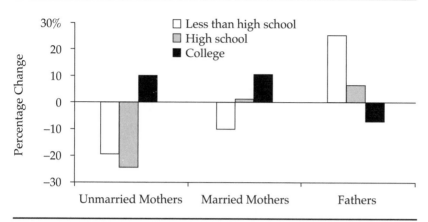

*Source:* Author's calculations of data from Census 2000, 6 percent sample (Ruggles et al. 2010b).

*Note:* For example, unmarried mothers with less than a high school education who have a disabled child are 19 percent less likely to be employed than unmarried mothers with less than a high school education whose child does not have a disability. All of these regression models include controls for mother's education, age, and number of children age zero to four and five to fifteen. All results shown are significant at $p < .05$.

10 percent lower than that of married mothers with a high school education whose child does not have a disability.

However, it is a different story for college-educated mothers: both married and unmarried college-graduate mothers who have a child with a disability are 10 percent *more* likely to be employed than are college-educated mothers whose children are not disabled.

There are a variety of possible explanations for these work patterns, and the reasons are complex. Less educated mothers earn less, so the potential family income loss is less if they do not work. However, their contributions to family income may be even harder to do without. Mothers with less than a high school education earn relatively little compared to the costs of child care; many of them can best support their families by staying home. More educated mothers often have careers rather than jobs, and these careers may have substantial penalties for frequent exits and re-entries. These college-educated mothers more often can afford special child care, including in-home care for a disabled child. They may also be better positioned to negotiate fathers' involvement in the care of that child. Thus, by continuing employment, many college-educated mothers of children with disabilities are able to maintain their higher incomes and more interesting jobs compared to less educated women.

The rates of employment of fathers with a disabled child depend on whether the wife is a full-time caregiver at home. Among men married to women who do not work, the fathers of children with disabilities are 19 percent more likely to be employed in the labor force than fathers of children without disabilities. This is because these fathers, regardless of their age, are more likely to devote themselves to work—they are less likely to be in school, less likely to be temporarily unemployed, and less likely to be on disability or to retire. This pattern suggests the greater gender role specialization (mothers as caregivers and fathers as breadwinners) that often happens when a child has a disability.

Many families at the Children's Rehabilitation Center report that the father's work limits his involvement in the daily life of his disabled child. An example of this is the case of Roger, the father of four-year-old Sadie, who has cerebral palsy with mild disabilities. Says Sadie's mother:

> He works very, very long [hours]. He travels a ton. When he's not travel-ing, he leaves in the morning at like six o'clock and he comes home at seven or eight o'clock at night everyday. So, yeah. Like, he's nice, like, he's emotionally supportive, but as far as like being there . . .

However, the increase in the rate of employment occurs primarily among less educated men, some of who might otherwise be out of the labor force. Among married fathers of children with disabilities whose wives do not work, those with less than a high school education are 25 percent more likely to be employed compared to similar fathers of children without disabilities, while 6 percent of fathers with high school diplomas are more likely to be employed. College-educated fathers of children with disabilities, in contrast, are 7 percent less likely to be employed than similarly educated fathers whose children do not have disabilities, perhaps because their wives are more successful at involving them in child care. Thus, one way less educated couples are able to handle the family needs for income and the special-care needs of their disabled children is for mothers to become full-time care providers, while men, upon whom families rely for income, are especially committed to employment.

For the college-educated, some type of shared arrangement between mothers and fathers for child care and for earnings is more likely. For example, sometimes both the fathers and the mothers have jobs with flexible schedules that allow them to work and share child care responsibilities, as described by Rita during her interview at the Children's Rehabilitation Center:

> Real estate. It's really flexible. . . . I work in the morning, and I take [my son] with me on appointments too sometimes . . . or my husband will take him to therapy, bring him to therapy . . . or my husband's home with him. So we . . . because my husband does the same thing . . . we're both in real estate. . . . I mean now if I was a single [parent], I don't know how I would do it.

Of course, potential earnings by fathers are an important consideration in whether mothers work, as Debra reports:

> I returned to work after [Ricky] was born. . . . We didn't have a diagnosis for him until he was, I think he was about two. . . . So I was working part-time when he started all this therapy. And then they wanted to increase the therapy so I decided to take a leave of absence to see if financially it could be done. . . . It could . . . so I left working. So that I could bring him to all his therapies.

Parents' decisions about employment change as their children age. Once a child enters school, many of the accommodations and therapies the child receives occur through special education rather than the health care system so that mothers have more time during the day when they are not caregivers (see chapter 7). This may make it more feasible for mothers of a seriously disabled child to work. This is especially common when a father is present to share child care before and after school. Working-class parents sometimes manage child care through shift-work, in which one parent is home while the other is at work (Presser 2003).

## The Decision to Have Another Child

For parents of a child with a disability, the decision to have another child is complex. They must decide whether they have the resources to care for another child, or if they should devote all of their energy to maximizing the well-being of the child with a disability. This is further complicated because of the risk that another child might also have a disability, stretching resources to the breaking point. In families in which the child with a disability is an only child, these issues are balanced by the desire to have another child who does not have a disability to "complete" their family. And there is the perceived need to have another child so that when the parents are gone, the adult child without a disability can care for the adult child with a disability.

Several parents interviewed at the Children's Rehabilitation Center mentioned these considerations. Debra, whose only child Ricky was born with a brain abnormality, is concerned that she and her husband might have another child with a disability, even though doctors say the chances are slight. Debra thinks they could not meet the specialized needs of two children with disabilities:

> Okay, it's extremely slight, so chances are it's not going to happen again. But what if it did? How are you going to meet both their needs? So then . . . if it didn't happen again, would it be fair to a baby to always be bringing a baby to [Ricky's] therapy? You know, because [Ricky is] going to be in therapy I'm sure for a very long time. So no, full attention, full focus on Ricky.

Parents sometimes choose to delay having another child until their child with the disability has less intensive needs. Gloria's daughter Emily was born with spina bifida. Gloria and her husband are examples of the greater flexibility parents have when their disabled child starts school. They did not have another child until Emily was eight: "I waited a certain amount of time where I felt I would have the capability and the time to spend with other children."

Andrea, age three, and Katie, age ten, both have an undiagnosed condition that causes spasticity. Katie attends regular school with a normal schedule, while Andrea, who has a lower tolerance for activities, only attends a regular preschool three mornings a week. Both daughters receive physical, occupational, and speech therapy twice a week through their local school system. Their parents, Carol and Mark, have always wanted a bigger family and would like to have a child who could go to college. They are considering a third child but are worried about another child having a disability:

> We're actually going to be starting adoption classes . . . we had originally thought infant, but now we're looking to adopt, like a twelve-, thirteen-year-old . . . I think we came to the point that our life's so crazy anyway, so why not? [Laughs] We have a lot to offer, so we just . . . we have a lot, home-wise, financially. We have a big house, we have extra room, we have the financial ability to send someone to college, so . . . we're like, well, why not look into it? And we always thought we wanted more children, so . . .

Other parents see benefits in having another child for their child with disabilities. Even though her current husband is not supportive, Loretta says it was good to have had a second child, both for herself

**Figure 3.4    Percentage of Mothers Having a Tubal Sterilization, by Months Since Birth and Disability Status of the Child**

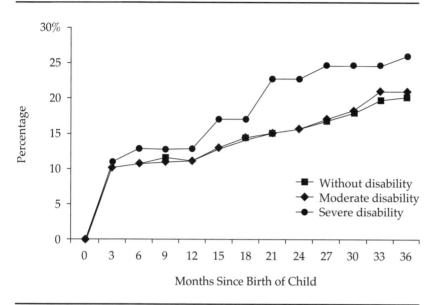

Months Since Birth of Child

*Source:* Park, Hogan, and Goldscheider (2003), reprinted with permission from John Wiley and Sons.
*Note:* Using these data and taking into account the interval since the first birth; the sex of the first child; the mother's age, marital status, education, employment; and an indicator of poverty status, the rate of second birth is lower among mothers of children with disabilities (odds ratio = 0.80, $p < .05$; MacInnes 2008).

and for her son Julian, who has a disability: "I notice that since I had the baby, [Julian had] been more open. And since I had the baby, it's like we opened up like . . . [Julian and I are] more close, how we communicate better. And, see, in fact the way that he treats the baby, I teach him . . . it's helped . . . it helped a lot."

These decisions show up in the matched information from the National Survey of Family Growth and the National Health Interview Survey. If their first child has a disability, the rate at which parents have a second child is about 20 percent less than among parents of children without disabilities.

Indeed, parents of a newborn child with a disability more often opt for permanent contraceptive measures to limit family size (figure 3.4). The rate of tubal sterilization in the months following the birth among mothers whose newborn infant has any disability is 65 percent higher than that of mothers whose newborns do not have disabilities (Park,

Hogan, and Goldscheider 2003). This type of tubal sterilization is nearly always elective surgery done for the purposes of preventing additional births. Mothers who give birth to a child with a serious disability are more likely to undergo sterilization once they learn their infant has a disability, consistent with what the mothers at the Children's Rehabilitation Center say. However, parents' plans for family size are unaffected by the presence of a child with a mild disability, even though a child with mild disabilities often can require extra resource commitments and create stress for families.

## Family Resources and the Economic Costs of a Disabled Child

Parents' marital and employment status, the severity of a child's disability, and the number of children in a family all have economic consequences for family life, but our findings did not specifically link children's medical condition and disability status to the poor economic situations of their families. Fortunately, the National Survey of Children with Special Health Care Needs asked families of children with special health care needs (both single-parent and two-parent households) about the economic impact of their child's medical condition (see figure 3.5).

While very few families of children who have special health care needs but no disability reported a family member quitting work, 14 percent of parents of children with serious disabilities and 22 percent of the families of children with severe disabilities reported that a parent left the paid labor force. As discussed earlier in this chapter, the person quitting work is almost always the mother. Those mothers of children with disabilities who do remain employed often reduce the number of hours at their jobs. For example, only 9 percent of parents of a child with special health care needs but no disability cut their work hours, compared to 27 percent of parents of children with mild disabilities and 44 percent of parents of children with severe disabilities.

According to the 2005–2007 American Community Survey for married couples with at least one child, when the mother of a child with a disability quits work and the husband continues to work at the same level, family income is about 29 percent less (the survey compares the family income for mothers with earnings with family income when mothers do not work). Thus, the caregiving needs of a child with a disability can lead to substantial reductions in family income. Single mothers of children with disabilities who need to quit work face a catastrophic income loss.

In addition, families raising children with disabilities need more income because of their child's health conditions. The dedicated costs of raising a child with a disability, even if the medical care is fully cov-

**Figure 3.5    Economic Experiences of Families by Disability Status of Children Under Eighteen**

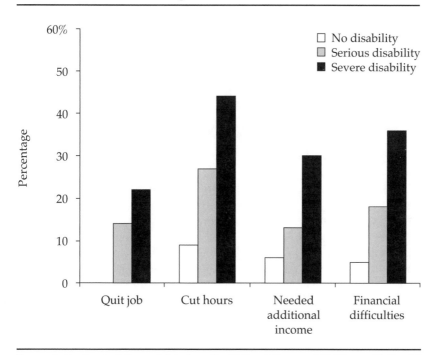

*Source:* Author's calculations of data from the National Survey of Children with Special Health Care Needs (U.S. Department of Health and Human Services 2005/2006).
*Note:* Survey includes children who have special health care needs but who do not have disabilities. All differences are significant at $p < .05$.

ered, are higher. Parents at the Children's Rehabilitation Center told us about some of the unusual costs that families bear as a direct result of their children's needs. Teresa said that as Sean has grown older, the family has needed to find the money to renovate their home in order to accommodate a bigger wheelchair:

> But now he's bigger, so they made the chair wider now, and he's hitting more things than he was before. So I had to take his bedroom door off. . . . Just to . . . make his bedroom bigger, build a bathroom, and bring my kitchen out will be $110,000.

Dan, the father of Scott, who has cerebral palsy, works multiple jobs to make ends meet. Even so, he says the family is chronically short of money due to the specialized care and modified home environment that Scott needs:

So the first five years, financially, I don't know how we did it. . . . I couldn't cut corners. I had four kids at home. I got a mortgage to pay. Braces were . . . so expensive. What do you say as a father? "No," when [my children] needed something? So if I didn't have the cash, I would charge it. And I still pay some debt now that I accumulated then.

Another father put the economic needs of his family this way: "So even if it couldn't be done, it was going to be done anyway."

The National Survey of Children with Special Health Care Needs shows that 13 percent of families of a child with a serious disability and 30 percent of families of a child with a severe disability say they need additional income for the specific purpose of medical care for their child with a disability.

This need for additional income, in combination with reduced earnings due to changes in patterns of employment, is linked to family financial difficulties. While only 5 percent of families of children with medical conditions but no disabilities have had financial difficulties due to their child's health condition, 18 percent of parents of a child with serious disabilities and 36 percent of parents of children with severe disabilities have financial difficulties that they say are the direct result of their child's disability. (These differences persist and are of similar magnitudes when logistic regression models for each outcome control for the age and sex of the child, family type, race and ethnicity, parents' education, region of residence, and metropolitan residence.) For some families the situation is dire: they sometimes cannot pay their monthly housing and utility bills, are in danger of losing their homes, and have inadequate income for other common family needs.

Thus, while all parents undergo changes in their relationship when they have a child, those changes are much more complex and largely negative when a child has a disability. Parents of children with disabilities more often end their relationships. They have fewer children than they might otherwise have had. They more often adopt traditional relationships in which the mother is the primary caregiver and the father is the breadwinner. They experience income loss and financial difficulties more frequently. This is especially true for parents of children with serious or severe disabilities, and it is more likely to occur in families in which the parents have less than a high school education. Despite these common patterns, other parents juggle work and family duties so that they share the caregiving and breadwinner responsibilities. If they are in jobs with flexible schedules, good wages, and good health insurance, they can get by economically. But it tends to be more educated parents who can find and afford care for their special-needs child. Single mothers of a child with a disability are not so fortunate—they tend to be full-time caregivers at home, are more often welfare-dependent, and often face dire economic circumstances.

The personal resources parents bring to their interpersonal relationships, their human capital, how capably they can manage their child's health care institutions, and the availability of structural support (such as flexible employment and family leave schedules) determine how parents' lives and relationships with each other are affected by having a child with a disability. The linked life courses of parents and their disabled children fully determine how families cope with the extra challenges they face.

# = Chapter 4 =

## Family Life, Social Support, and Religious Activities

AMILIES' ABILITY to raise children depends a great deal upon the
social and economic resources that are available to them. On average, children who grow up with two parents have access to greater
financial resources than children growing up in one-parent families.
Family poverty increases food insecurity and reduces housing quality
while indirectly affecting children by increasing family stress and con-
straining parental behavior (Engle and Black 2008). Parents with higher
levels of education can usually avoid the harmful effects of poverty, as
households containing one or two parents with at least a high school
diploma are less likely to be in chronic poverty than families with less
than a high school diploma. Among those already living in poverty,
parents who are more highly educated are better able to claim all of the
benefits for which their family qualifies.

Yet children with disabilities more often grow up in disadvantaged
family circumstances. The Census shows that a third of children with
disabilities live in one-parent households, compared to about 25 percent
of children without disabilities. Parents of children with disabilities are
also more likely to have less than a high school diploma (18 percent)
than parents of children without disabilities (12 percent). Twenty-nine
percent of families of children with disabilities live in poverty, compared to 19 percent of the families of children without disabilities.

Living in poverty makes it more likely that a child will also live in a
dangerous neighborhood. Safe neighborhoods exert a powerful influence on children's development (Brooks-Gunn et al. 1993). Exposure to
neighborhood violence has a variety of negative emotional and behavioral effects on young people. Additionally, poor or dangerous local
neighborhood conditions also are associated with reduced physical activity among children, as parental perceptions of neighborhood safety
shape children's leisure time activities.

The National Longitudinal Survey of Youth (which includes only
those children who are able to complete an interview, as noted earlier)
uses a measure called the Physical Environment Risk Index to deter-

mine whether or not a neighborhood provides a stable environment for an adolescent to grow up within. A safe neighborhood is based on an interviewer's observation that buildings on the street where the adolescent lives are "well kept" or "fairly well kept," on the fact that the interviewer did not fear for his or her own safety when visiting the adolescent's residence, and on the adolescent's reports that gunshots are not heard in their neighborhood in a typical week (Moore et al. 1999). Youth with disabilities are about 30 percent less likely than youth without disabilities to live in a safe neighborhood.

## Shared Family Activities

Well-functioning families are organized around common, shared activities and routines. Families of adolescent children with disabilities have daily routines much like those of other families of adolescent children who do not have disabilities. The National Longitudinal Survey of Youth indicates that on average these families eat a meal together at least five days each week, participate in some type of family activities at home or outside of the home about three days each week, and spend between one and two days each week engaged in some type of religion-related activities. While there are few differences in the frequency of these family routines, the interviews suggest it is quite likely that there are bigger differences when the children with disabilities are young. Moreover, the content and meaning of these activities assume greater importance when a child has a disability. For families of children with disabilities, shared dinners are a chance to show that all children and both parents are committed to one another and that their child with a disability is a fully integrated member of the family with a special place in their lives.

In many ways, having a child with a disability may actually strengthen family life. The parents we talked to at the Children's Rehabilitation Center told us that, in contrast to other families, they spend most of their free time at home with family. An example is Peggy, who gets home early from work so that she can meet her daughter Stephanie's bus and cook dinner for the family. The family eats together most nights. They often watch favorite television shows or rent movies to watch together. Peggy reports that her other daughters have sports and after-school activities, but these are not excuses for missing the family dinner.

The style and content of many other routines almost certainly differ for families with disabled children, even at the most basic levels. A family that needs to accommodate a child with dietary restrictions may wind up organizing shopping and meals for the entire family to avoid gluten, dairy, or high-carbohydrate foods. Children who lack the ability to feed themselves will likely join the family at the table but will be spoon-fed by a family member. When a child is restricted to a wheelchair, the family will need to plan outings carefully to ensure that a destination is accessible, to identify parking, and to locate appropriate entrances and seating.

Families of children with behavioral difficulties are more likely to think carefully about which settings will be most accommodating to their children and where noise and disruptive behavior is more the norm than the exception. These families also need to plan vacations that, in addition to fitting in with reduced travel budgets, will accommodate their children. For example, they may try to avoid long auto or airplane rides, extensive foot travel, or lodgings that do not have cooking facilities. These vacation spots typically are places in which all children and their parents can have fun together, but where the children without disabilities can roam more freely with at least some independence to do other activities they enjoy.

### Parents' Social Lives

While family life may be strengthened when a child has a disability, parents' social lives and friendships are likely to change dramatically. Karen says that she lost all of her friends after her son Brandon was born:

> All the ones [friends] I had before he was born are gone. My best friend, Molly, won't call me anymore. She says I have no time for her. They don't understand . . . why I have to take him with me, and they can't deal with the things that he does, or how he looks.

The situation can be especially difficult for families when they are from ethnic groups or immigrant communities that may have limited experience with children with disabilities. Patrice, an immigrant from Ghana, describes this painful situation:

> You know, something funny happened to me when I had Nick. Well, we used to go to a church, but I stopped because . . . well, you know the funny thing about Africans . . . some people believe like in witches and all that, and . . . some of the people that we knew in the church, when I had Nick, they were all . . . afraid, like, "Oh, maybe you did something and now God is punishing you!" or "Maybe you did something to somebody in Ghana and they make voodoo on you!"

However, a recurrent theme among parents we interviewed was that new friendships form, often with other parents of children with disabilities. As Ricky's mother said:

> It's very funny because you meet new friends that have children with disabilities. I've become pretty friendly with this little boy's mom who went to preschool with Ricky. . . . The people with the special-needs kids are more down to earth maybe. More realistic.

This suggests that couples may have a smaller network of friends than before, but they can rely more upon the friends they do have, even for exceptional kinds of support. At the same time, new friends whose children also have disabilities may expand their support networks. Yet the National Survey of Children's Health indicates that mothers of children with disabilities are slightly less likely than other mothers to have someone they can turn to for emotional support with their parenting (86 percent compared to 91 percent of other mothers). Mothers raising children with disabilities are also slightly less likely to feel there are adults in their neighborhood who can be trusted to help if their child is in trouble (66 percent compared to 71 percent of mothers of children without disabilities). Thus, while most families with children have sources of social support they can call on for day-to-day help and emotional support, this type of aid differs and sometimes is not enough for parents raising children with disabilities.

## Reduced Time for Social Activities

The National Survey of Children with Special Health Care Needs shows that the availability of parents raising children with disabilities for social activities is often restricted by the need to provide special medical care at home (figure 4.1). Parents of the healthiest children in that survey typically spend less than one hour per week providing medical care at home (61 percent); one-third spend between one and ten hours. Fewer than 7 percent of these parents spend more than eleven hours per week providing medical care at home. In contrast, 29 percent of families of children with severe disabilities devote eleven or more hours each week to home medical care; in fact, one-fifth of families with a child with severe disabilities spend more than twenty hours each week giving medical care at home (tabulation not shown in figure). This is a stark reminder of the amount of time that families of children with severe disabilities devote to their children's health care needs at home.

The National Survey of Children with Special Health Care Needs

**Figure 4.1    Hours per Week Spent on Children's Home Health Care by Children's Disability Status, Children Age Under Eighteen**

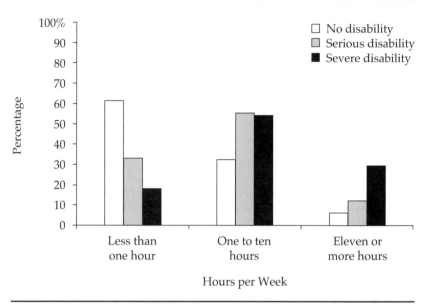

*Source:* Author's calculations of data from the National Survey of Children with Special Health Care Needs (U.S. Department of Health and Human Services 2005/2006).
*Notes:* Survey includes children who have special health care needs but who do not have disabilities. An ordered logistic regression controlling for race, poverty level, mother's education, number of children and adults, size of place of residence, and sex and age of the child shows that the intensity of child medical care is increased dramatically (odds ratio [OR] = 2.89, $p < .001$, for parents of a seriously disabled child; and OR = 6.70, $p < .001$, for parents of a child with a severe disability).

shows that parents of disabled children often find themselves spending significant time scheduling and coordinating professional care (tabulations not shown). While only one-quarter of parents of children with chronic health conditions but no disabilities spend more than one hour per week managing and coordinating medical care outside of the home, two-thirds of families of children with severe disabilities do so. In fact, the burdens of this activity can be extreme: 8 percent of families of children with severe disabilities report spending more than ten hours per week coordinating their children's medical care. It is easy to see how parents can be overwhelmed by this task.

Of course, parents who are more economically secure are better able to hire specialists to come into the home to help with their children's health care needs. Some families with sufficient financial resources arrange specialized daycare that takes care of their children's medical needs outside of the home setting. They also are better able to afford visiting nurses and physical or occupational therapists at home. Thus, among parents of children with severe disabilities, only one-fifth who are college graduates spend more than ten hours per week on home health care, compared to 43 percent of parents who have less than a high school education.

## Support Networks

In the face of these caregiving challenges, support from extended family can be crucial for parents of children with disabilities. Grandparents, in particular, are often a potential source of support for families with chronic special needs or during times of crisis. A few of the families at the Children's Rehabilitation Center told us that a grandmother lives in the household to assist with the daily care of their grandchild and with homemaker tasks. One mother reported:

> My mom was working so I never bothered her to babysit. Never asked her to do anything. It was just me and my husband. And then she retired and she's home doing nothing. I was like, "Mom, you can come and stay with us," . . . so she came and stayed with us. So when my husband's not around, she's the second parent.

Such an arrangement is not very common, however. Families raising children with one or more serious disabilities are only slightly less likely than families whose children are without disabilities to have a grandparent living with them. However, grandparents are 28 percent more likely to be the primary source of child care outside of the home when a child has one or more serious disabilities. It may be that the in-home care needs for a disabled grandchild are too stressful for many grandparents. This is the case when home care requires special skills, such as knowing how to respond to autistic behaviors; adhering to dietary restrictions; and giving injections of medications, oxygen therapies, and catheters. These concerns are likely to be less (or at least of shorter duration) for grandparents providing before- or after-school care. This desire to provide extra support and the possible related stress sometimes shows up in the relationship between grandparents and their grandchildren—grandparents of children with disabilities are half as likely to establish a close relationship with their grandchildren compared to grandparents of children who do not have any disabilities (Park, Hogan, and D'Ottavi 2004). (These findings, from the matched data, are net of the age and sex of the child, number of siblings, number of living grandparents, number of parents in the home, socioeconomic status, and ethnicity.)

Nonetheless, many parents of disabled children receive regular support from friends and family members, as our interviews confirm. Erin's mother, Marilyn, says:

> We have fantastic extended family on both sides. . . . Robert's mom and dad is right across the street. My parents are ten minutes away and they all have been extremely dedicated to her. I couldn't ask for a better family on both sides.

Kimberly also says her family's help has been crucial in taking care of Nathan:

> My grandmother is still living. . . . She lives a couple of blocks away . . . so she watched him for me, and she still does . . . and my dad's there. I just have a lot of family support.

Patrice (an immigrant from Africa) was surprised at how much help she has received from friends as well as family:

> People that we don't expect, you know, like we have black and white friends . . . people that we were not expecting that they would help, they were the one helping.

Other parents are confident that support will be there when they need it. As Emily's mother, Gloria, remarks:

> So there's just that comfort level . . . you know if I need somebody to spend the night, you know. . . . So, like, my brother would spend the night or my niece or I have a friend, a close friend that will come out and we have a good support system.

Of course, grandparents who live more than an hour of travel away from their adult children are generally unable to assist with daily child care for grandchildren. In this case, many of our respondents report that grandparents sometimes provide respite for parents by taking care of their grandchild for several days or more.

However, some parents find very little assistance when it comes to their relatives. Laura, who is from Guatemala, gets no family support because her extended family lives far away:

> I think it's that when you come to this country you lose your relations and your love and care, so we just live—me, my husband, and my three kids—so we live our own life and everybody else lives theirs.

There are also those families whose relatives, though living nearby, are of no help. For example, Connie, the widowed mother of a child with severe cerebral palsy (who has weak motor skills, has cognitive limitations, and is unable to talk), said, "My mother totally ignores Eric. It's just her own problem. She can't bond with him so doesn't deal with him." Amelia's mother, Susan, complains about her parents' attitude:

> My parents, they were kind of there when it suited their . . . they're kind of selfish. . . . When it was time for them [to winter] in Florida . . . they called us from their camper as they drove. . . . We were in the hospital, they called for Amelia to wave at them as their camper went by the window.

In still other situations, some mothers are unhappy with what might be described as the "help" they receive from their husbands' family. As Karen, Brandon's mother, complains:

> They actually make things worse. I do not like my mother-in-law; I do not like my husband's family. They make things a lot worse. When I'm down there, I'm even more miserable because they're always, "Why are you giving him that medicine? Why are you doing that?" . . . And it makes it harder.

Given all the difficulties and disadvantages encountered by families raising children with disabilities, it is not surprising that they are prone to stress and anxiety. Population data from the National Survey of Children's Health confirm that raising children with disabilities is stressful. Nearly one-quarter of mothers of children with disabilities report thinking that their child is usually or always more difficult than other children, in contrast to only 4 percent of mothers of children without disabilities. More than one-half of mothers raising children with disabilities say that they sacrifice more for their child than most parents, compared to one-quarter of mothers raising a child without a disability. However, most mothers are able to handle these stresses. Compared to mothers of children who have health conditions but no disabilities (10 percent), the percentage of mothers who experience high levels of anxiety is increased to 13 percent if their children are somewhat limited by disabilities, and to 19 percent (odds ratio = 1.94; $p < .05$) if their children are seriously limited by disabilities for mothers of children with serious disabilities, controlling for race, education of the mother, age of the mother, number of children, and family poverty status. These difficulties in parenting children with disabilities and their mothers' high levels of anxiety mean that a somewhat greater percentage of mothers of children with disabilities report they are unhappy with their lives.

Many families of children with disabilities find solace and support in religious activities. Church is often not only a place of worship and community but somewhere that families pray for strength to deal with the special challenges they face, pray together with their church community for the well-being of their disabled child, and participate in one of the few community groups that tries to welcome all persons regardless of their behaviors or disabilities. While the frequency of religion-related activities is not higher among families that include adolescent children with disabilities, the parents we interviewed often described their churches as places of refuge where all members of the family are equally welcomed and treated with respect. Typically, churches are handicapped-accessible as well. Churches are also places where parents, especially stay-at-home parents, can meet other adults and maintain social ties.

Paul, who has cerebral palsy with many complications, loves going to church and participating in activities. Recently, he interacted with his pastor in a joint sermon, and Paul shared his blessings and joy of life. Paul practiced repeatedly with his parents, a speech coach, and the pastor before the big day. On the day of the sermon, his speech coach was connected through a microphone in Paul's ear and helped prompt him about what he wanted to say. This sermon was a fine portrayal of how persons who may be seen as terribly handicapped by outsiders can nevertheless express their sense of God's love for them, the many blessings they have, joy, and gratitude for family.

Families feel the blessings, too. It is hard, if not impossible, in a book of this sort to capture the extraordinary love that family members have for their children with disabilities. Despite their many sacrifices, not a single mother at the Children's Rehabilitation Center suggested they would be better off if they had not had their child, nor did any say they would like to have their preschool- or school-age child live in a long-term-care facility. I have never met any parent of a child with a disability who is less than fully loving and caring for their child to the best of their abilities. Indeed, most parents of children with disabilities are proud of what the children have accomplished, see their family lives positively, and cannot understand why others would see them differently.

This love is perhaps most obvious when a child with a severe disability dies. Well-meaning friends and family may think—and perhaps even comment—that the parents will be "better off" because the extraordinary challenges they face have now ended. The parents and the brothers and sisters have a much different perspective, however; they grieve deeply the loss of a special and beloved family member. After a child with a disability is gone, families that have met the challenges of raising a child with a disability express considerable satisfaction and pride with the way their family came together to support their family member with special needs. The parents of Christina, who died of Rett syndrome, wrote:

> On January 30, 2006, our beautiful daughter lost her battle with Rett syndrome at the age of thirteen, due to the devastating complications of this cruel disease. Our family continues to be involved and supportive of efforts to educate, bring awareness and hope to families. . . . We miss our sweet Christina, her smile, laugh, and her kisses. She illuminated our lives.

# = Chapter 5 =

## Parents, Adolescent Children with Disabilities, and the Transition to Adulthood[1]

A<small>LL PARENTS</small> face the challenges of helping their children navigate adolescence and young adulthood. This is particularly difficult for parents raising children with disabilities, as parents may have to modify their expectations for their children's participation in adult life. As Margaret, the mother of David (who has cerebral palsy with mobility limitations and learning disabilities), explained: "There were a lot of unknowns in the beginning. . . . Even now, will David ever be able to [finish high school and] live independently by himself? We don't know. We would like to think he will. But we don't know for sure." Danielle, the mother of Ricky (who has severe developmental disabilities and limitations in his fine motor skills and speech), said, "The hardest part is not being able to plan. Not knowing what to expect, not knowing where he's going to be."

The impact of health impairments on children's abilities to do everyday activities and participate fully in social roles varies greatly even among children with the same potentially disabling medical condition. Nonetheless, while parents of children with disabilities are less sanguine about their child's prospects for adult life than parents of children without disabilities, they hope—and in some cases, anticipate—that their children will lead self-sufficient adult lives. Jacqui's mother, Amanda, foresees a fulfilling future for her daughter, despite Jacqui's cerebral palsy and use of a cane, but anticipates that she will require more help than other children: "I'd like [Jacqui] to go to college . . . and she wants to. . . . I'm trying to think of a job that she could do easily with her disability, and . . . I expect her to get married and have a family and everything. . . . It'd be a little hard, but I think she can do it." Sadie has cognitive limitations and disabilities with gross motor skills but is able to attend a regular school. Tara, her mother, is positive about her daughter's future despite her cognitive issues:

It's my hope that, you know, she's going to be able to overcome, like you know, especially any cognitive issues that may present themselves . . . She's got a really like strong personality . . . And I like to think that by and large she's going to be able to be what she wants or do what she wants.

## Raising Independent Children

Most of the parents we spoke to express the hope that their children will someday be able to manage their own disabilities. As Harry's mother, Janet, explains, his disability (which resulted from a stroke in utero) can be managed in the long term with a commitment to a physical therapy regimen: "But, I mean, he's going to have to do this for the rest of his life. Even when he's twenty, thirty, forty, fifty . . . he's always going to have to do the exercises. . . . I think he's going to be fine because he's going to have to be." Karen, the mother of Brandon (who has Duchene muscular dystrophy), says:

> We're hoping that he can live on his own. [We will] try to get him into a group home situation so he can be self-sufficient and not like his aunt [who has Down syndrome and] depends on the family. [We'd] rather him be self-sufficient. . . . If not, then we know that he will be with us.

Sometimes children are more independent than their parents anticipate. Andrew, who is fourteen years old, lost both legs to bacterial meningitis when he was six. Against his mother's advice, Andrew "put on [in]-line skates on his prosthetic legs, crawled to their white picket fence, and spent hours each day holding on to it to teach him[self] to skate. . . . Andrew [now] does extreme-biking, snowboarding, and dirt-biking . . . Andrew [tells people] he does not get depressed; he prefers to think about what he's got instead of what he's lost."

Matt, who has Down syndrome, could also be surprisingly independent, although not in such a constructive fashion, as his sister Sally describes:

> When he was a little boy, he would chase birds wherever we were, and he would take off on us if we weren't watching him very closely. As he grew into his early teens . . . he would sneak off to [the family's] barn and chase the horses. . . . The horses responded by circling around the barn at nearly full speed, kicking their heels. It was a fright to go to the barn and see Matt amidst the flying dust and racing horses.

**Figure 5.1    Children Who Are Victims of Bullying, by Disability
Status and Age**

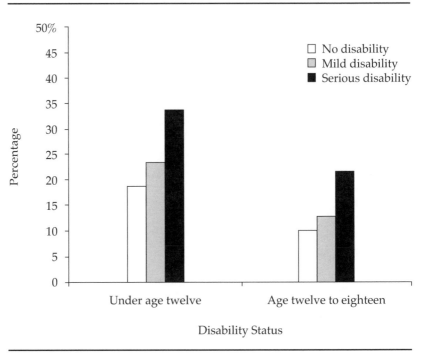

Disability Status

*Source:* Author's calculations of data from the National Longitudinal Survey of Youth
(U.S. Bureau of Labor Statistics 1997).

## Bullying

All parents must balance young people's need for independence with
the need to keep them safe. Young people with disabilities, especially
those with serious disabilities, are more likely to be bullied than children without disabilities and may encounter bullying in many situations: between home and school, in school, and in the homes of other
children. Figure 5.1 shows the prevalence of bullying by age and disability status (among children sampled in the National Longitudinal
Survey of Youth [NLSY] who were able to be interviewed). Only 19
percent of children without disabilities say they were bullied before
their twelfth birthday, compared to 23 percent of children with mild
disabilities and 34 percent of children with serious disabilities who report being bullied. Between the ages of twelve to eighteen, these patterns of bullying continue—10 percent of children without disabilities

report bullying, versus 13 percent of children with mild disabilities and 21 percent of children with serious disabilities.

This pattern of bullying of children with disabilities is especially troubling for parents, since it may portend a lifetime of derogatory or unfair treatment by peers. As being bullied is also associated with poorer relationships with classmates, more difficultly in making friends, and loneliness, this is a serious and multifaceted problem that parents often cannot resolve.

## Adolescent Behaviors

In addition to the greater risk of bullying, parents of children with disabilities also face other challenges as their children enter adolescence and are prone to more dangerous behavior. The NLSY allows me to investigate the percentage of children who run away from home and to examine whether they have less safe relationships with peers and greater participation in dangerous activities and risky sexual behaviors. (Again, keep in mind that the NLSY does not include children with the most severe cognitive disabilities, since adolescents in the survey must be able to participate in an interview.)

### Running Away from Home

Running away from home is detrimental for young people, as runaway youth are more likely to be involved with deviant peer groups, criminal activity, and drug use. In fact, runaway behavior during adolescence is associated with addictive substance abuse, victimization, and incarceration later in adulthood. This is a particularly dangerous behavior for children with disabilities, since they may be less able to handle interpersonal negotiations in an unstructured setting. In addition, children with disabilities often have special needs for medications, access to medical care, equipment, and diets that are unlikely to be available for runaways.

Children with disabilities are more likely than children without disabilities to run away from home by age eleven: 18 percent of children without disabilities report running away, compared to 26 percent of children with mild disabilities and 31 percent of children with serious disabilities (the NLSY classifies children as running away from home if they have "left home and stayed away at least overnight without [their] parent's prior knowledge or permission"). The situation improves somewhat as children get older: only 10 percent of children without disabilities report running away from home between the ages of twelve and eighteen, compared to 22 percent of children with serious disabilities.

## Dangers of "Hanging Out" and Negative Peer Interaction

As children become adolescents, they are more likely to "hang out," spend time cruising in a car with other teens, or attend events where there may not be any adult supervision (such as drinking parties or popular music concerts). While all parents worry as their children become more independent, the situation is especially troubling for parents whose children have limitations in their abilities to interact on an equal footing with peers. Moreover, some children with disabilities, particularly those with conditions such as autism or ADHD, are impulsive and less able to make careful judgments about safety.

Peer interactions among adolescents can lead to the use of alcohol, tobacco, and drugs and to other risky and delinquent behaviors. Taking into account associated family factors, the NLSY (which includes only adolescents able to respond to a survey and thus excludes the severely cognitively impaired) indicates that adolescents with disabilities are no more likely to use tobacco or alcohol by age eighteen and are only slightly more likely to use marijuana than their non-disabled peers. However, adolescents with disabilities are much more likely to engage in other types of delinquent behaviors.

The Index of Delinquency is constructed for all respondents to the NLSY to measure behaviors they have experienced by age sixteen (Moore et al. 1999). The index is a summary measure of delinquency that includes ten types of behaviors: running away from home, destruction of property, other property crime, theft (under $50 and over $50), assault, gang membership, carrying a handgun, selling drugs, and police arrest. This index ranges from a low of 0 to a high of 10. Children without disabilities have a delinquency index of 1.5, compared to 1.9 for adolescents with mild disabilities and 2.4 for those with serious disabilities.

Parents' concerns about peer interactions are evident when they are asked about the potential of serious legal difficulties. Only 3 percent of parents whose child does not have a disability believe that there is greater than a one-in-four chance their child will end up in jail, compared to 7 percent of parents of children with mild disabilities and 15 percent of parents of children with serious disabilities.

Shannon explains her worries about how her son Andrew (who has a disability that limits coordination, verbal skills, motor skills, motor planning, visual perception, and understanding of nonverbal cues) engages with peers: "It is good that he is not geeky, which is what we thought he would be when he was growing up. But he so not wants to be like that. . . . He wants to be cool . . . which is troubling because it leads you down this whole other pathway with [peer] interactions."

## Unprepared for Sex

Many parents of adolescent children have difficulty thinking about their children's sexual development and activities. A large percentage of parents are unaware of or underestimate their children's sexual activity, especially at young ages. This may be especially the case for parents of children with disabilities. Although many of the parents interviewed at the Children's Rehabilitation Center want and expect their children to marry and become parents, this is seldom connected to a discussion of sexual development, choice of partner, contraceptive use, or prevention of sexually transmitted diseases—topics of great importance to parents of children without disabilities. Unlike parents of most children, the parents of children with disabilities talked about their children's marriage and parenting futures without ever mentioning their children dating, their children having girlfriends or boyfriends, or teaching their children about disease prevention or contraception. The topic seems to be something that many parents of adolescents with disabilities have simply not thought about.

Some parents have thought about this, though, and in rare cases, their concerns are not a child's sexual maturation but a lack thereof. Nick's parents worry a great deal about Nick's sexual development. Nick has Prader-Willi syndrome, a congenital disorder caused by a chromosomal defect that is characterized by sexual infantilism, mental handicap, obsessive eating, and obesity. Nick's mother Patricia worries what he will do when he learns his limitations: "Oh, I want him to go to school, and I want him to be able to take care of himself. . . . I think the hardest thing will be difficult for me is telling him you can't have children or you can't have sex, you know, because they are . . . how do you, how will I . . . their sexual area is so underdeveloped."

Nevertheless, sexual precocity is particularly common among girls with disabilities, whose initial sexual experiences are more likely to happen at younger ages, are less likely to occur in romantic relationships, and are more likely to involve a partner who is at least six years older. Among those adolescents who are sexually active, the NLSY shows that initial sexual intercourse occurs at age sixteen or younger for 53 percent of girls with serious disabilities, compared to 39 percent of young women without disabilities. Adolescent girls sometimes have first sexual intercourse with a boy with whom they have no romantic relationships; this is the case for 37 percent of girls with a serious disability but only 30 percent of girls without a disability. Twenty-one percent of girls with serious disabilities report that their first sexual partner is six or more years older, as opposed to only 16 percent of girls with mild disabilities and 8 percent of girls without disabilities. The reasons for these differences in sexual experiences may include victimization and efforts on the child's part to gain attention, but clearly parents of daughters with disabilities are even more likely to have difficulties with their daughters' sexual relationships than other parents.

Given the developmental significance of early sexual experience for all young persons, this is a matter of serious concern for parents of children with disabilities. Girls who have sex when they are sixteen or younger with a man who is six years older would, in many states, be considered victims of statutory rape. Parents of daughters with disabilities thus encounter more difficulties than other parents in promoting responsible and respectful sexual activities as a normal part of adolescent development and in protecting their daughters from sexual predators. This is exacerbated by the difficulties their children sometimes face in negotiating relationships with peers.

## Parents' Promotion of Education

One way that parents prepare their children for adult life is by helping them develop educational and occupational goals. These aspirations confront reality, however, when adolescents face educational hurdles specific to their disability status. The NLSY traces the educational experiences of adolescents and young adults. Children with disabilities have much poorer performance in schools than children without disabilities. Children with serious disabilities are three times more likely than children without disabilities to repeat a year of schooling and three times more likely to take remedial courses. In fact, children with disabilities are much less likely to complete high school than other children—by ages eighteen to twenty-two, 89 percent of children without disabilities graduate from high school, compared to 79 percent of children with mild disabilities and 65 percent of children with serious disabilities. Taking into account their more disadvantaged family origins, weaker school performance, and lower expectations for college enrollment, the odds of children with serious disabilities graduating from high school are only 53 percent as high as those of children without disabilities (Shandra and Hogan 2009).

The completion of high school is critical for successful entry into the adult workforce. High school graduation is an important signal to potential employers that young adults who may look or act differently from other job applicants still have intellectual, organizational, and social skills comparable to those of other high school graduates. Also, secondary school completion is important for young persons with disabilities that prevent physical labor. Thus, lower high school graduation rates of children with disabilities may presage lifetime dependency on parents. That children with serious disabilities are frequently unable to graduate with high school diplomas, often despite the best efforts of their parents, is an indication of the difficulties parents face in preparing their children with disabilities for adulthood. It also is the first indication for children with disabilities that their educational or career aspirations may be unattainable.

In today's economy, a college education is the best predictor that young adults will hold jobs that offer health care benefits, some job security, and good salaries. Parents' expectations that their children will complete college are 16 percent lower ($p < .05$) if their child has a serious disability compared to those of parents whose children do not have disabilities (Shandra and Hogan 2009).[2]

Among high school graduates, 70 percent of children without disabilities and 60 percent of children with mild disabilities begin college ($p < .05$), compared to only 31 percent of children with serious disabilities ($p < .05$), primarily because children with disabilities who graduate from high school have lower academic performance and college aspirations and fewer social and economic resources than their peers without disabilities. Holding these traits constant, we find that they are able to enroll in college at the same rate as children without disabilities. (This analysis is based on a logistic regression model using prospective data on educational attainment, with controls for family origins, race-ethnicity, and academic performance.) This suggests that children with disabilities are not less likely to enroll in college as a result of limitations in mobility, self-care, or hearing and speaking, per se. Rather, they are less likely to enroll in college because learning and behavioral disabilities negatively affect their academic performance in high school, limit their aspirations, and decrease the likelihood they will graduate from high school. Given these findings, the focus should be on promoting programs to enable children with disabilities, particularly at the high school level.

*Different Parental Roles and Enforcement*    At the family level, mothers of children with disabilities are often the ones to help their adolescents with disabilities focus on independent activities and schoolwork. Mothers more often see themselves as "enforcers," while fathers are more lax.

Harry's mother mentions that she rewards positive behaviors: "I make him work for everything he gets. That's the hard part." Erin's mother, Marilyn, says she is more demanding than Erin's father: "I'm more, 'You got to do your homework. And you have to take pride in the final product. Look how neat the paper looks . . . ' Where [her father] is more, 'Oh, don't be so hard. . . . Just get it on paper so we can [go] bike riding.'" Nina, the mother of Vanessa, reports similar differences with her husband: "He's the softie. He gives in to her."

Such "enforcement" contributes to the quality of parent and child relationships in adolescence, which are essential for children to make successful transitions to adulthood and are associated with many other positive family processes that contribute to later well-being. The Parent-Youth Relationship Scale, a section within the larger NLSY survey, is based on adolescents' responses to eight items: adolescents (1) think highly of parents, (2) want to be like their parents, and (3) enjoy spending time with their parents; and if they perceive their parents as (4) praising them for doing well, (5) not criticizing them or their ideas, (6) doing things important to them, (7) not blaming them for the parents' problems, and (8) not making and canceling plans for no good reason. The scale has a range from 0 (least favorable) to 8 (most favorable).

There is a small but interesting difference in the structure of parent-child relationships when the children describe the quality of their relationships with their mothers and fathers. While fathers' relationships to children are not significantly affected by a child's disability status either positively or negatively, mothers' relationships with their children are 1.7 points lower on the relationship scale if the child has a serious disability. This is an important finding, since children without disabilities have closer relationships with their mothers, but it suggests that adolescents with disabilities may resent their mothers' stricter discipline.

## Finding Work

Beyond educational attainment, work is essential to adult social status, as well as giving access to economic resources for residential independence and family formation, and integration in an environment with defined roles that, when accomplished, enhance individuals' sense of efficacy and self-worth. Accordingly, a successful school-to-work transition is essential for young persons with disabilities if they are to fully participate in adult society. At the same time, this transition has historically been particularly difficult for persons with disabilities, in part because of physical and social barriers to employment, as well as the lack of special accommodations to enable persons with limitations to do productive work.

In recent years, federal, state, and local governments and private businesses have created some employment opportunities for young adults with disabilities. School systems and employers have become more accommodating of the special needs of people with disabilities and have created opportunities for employment and provided support for workers with disabilities (Blackorby and Wagner 1996). At the same time, parents recognize that significant barriers to employment remain, especially when their children have serious disabilities. According to the Census, the reality that parents and children confront is that only 28 percent of young persons with physical disabilities are working by ages eighteen to twenty-four, compared to 52 percent of persons without physical disabilities (Hogan and Lichter 1995).

An alternative strategy for promoting children's economic success is school-to-work programs that can lead to employment immediately following high school. In the NLSY study, 52 percent of all children with disabilities who attend high school are enrolled in school-based programs such as cooperative education or technical preparation, and 35 percent are enrolled in workplace-based programs that include internships or apprenticeships, job shadowing, and mentoring.

School-based programs increase the odds that young adults with disabilities will complete high school. Research suggests that while many of these programs confer long-term benefits for employment, cooperative education, which combines academic and vocational studies with a job in a related field, is most consistently related to positive work outcomes. Compared to young people with disabilities who are not in these programs, young people who participate in these programs increase their likelihood of full-time employment by 21 percent and their likelihood that a job provides health insurance and sick leave by 26 percent (although this analysis did not include less cognitively able adolescents who are unable to participate in an interview). Such programs also increase annual income. Participation in employer-sponsored programs also increases the odds that disabled young people will get jobs that provide health insurance and paid sick days. For young people with disabilities who do find work, both school-based programs and work-based programs are advantageous compared to other general education programs for children with disabilities (Shandra and Hogan 2008).

## *The Transition to Adulthood*

Despite the fact that high school graduation, employment, and economic independence are enhanced by participation in these types of enterprises, the transition to adulthood is far less favorable for young persons with learning disabilities or with a combination of physical, behavioral, and learning disabilities that qualify them for special education status (Wells, Sandefur, and Hogan 2004). The National Longitudinal Transition Study of Special Education Students interviewed parents of special education students—those with learning disabilities or some combination of learning, behavioral, and physical disabilities—and followed up to learn about children's adult roles in additional parent interviews five years later. Comparing eighteen- to twenty-six-year-old men who were in special education when they were in secondary school to other young men in the National Education Longitudinal Survey, I find that only 14 percent of the special education students were enrolled in post-secondary education, compared to 71 percent of students without disabilities (the results are similar for young women with disabilities). Instead of continuing their education, special education students were more likely to be working and living with their parents in the years immediately after high school (35 percent versus 16 percent of youth without disabilities).

Moreover, 44 percent of these male special education students were very dependent on their families (living at home, not enrolled in school, and not working) as they entered the post–high school years, compared to only 5 percent of other young men. These differences are least among young men who have hearing, vision, or mobility problems. Young men who are classified as cognitively disabled or have multiple disabilities typically remain fully dependent on their families in the post–high school period.

However, persons who have profound cognitive limitations can still participate in adult roles, albeit in other ways. Sheltered workshops can help employ young adults who lack the skills to work in the formal economy. Many people with Down syndrome work as cleaners, in restaurant jobs, or in many other office jobs (as store clerks or mail room employees, for instance). It is likely that many young persons with other severe disabilities could be similarly productive if they were given the training and opportunity that is now standard for children with Down syndrome. According to the Census, young persons with disabilities (regardless of severity) generally seem to get more settled into adult roles by ages twenty-five through thirty-four, but their disadvantages are considerable (see figure 5.2).

By these ages, more than 20 percent of young adults classified as having disabilities still lived with their parents, compared to only 10 percent of young adults without disabilities. Four-fifths of young adults without disabilities were in the labor force (working or looking for work) compared to only 57 percent of those with mobility limitations, 35 percent of those with self-care limitations, 48 percent of those with

**Figure 5.2    Adult Life Experiences by Disability Status, Persons Age
Twenty-five to Thirty-two Years**

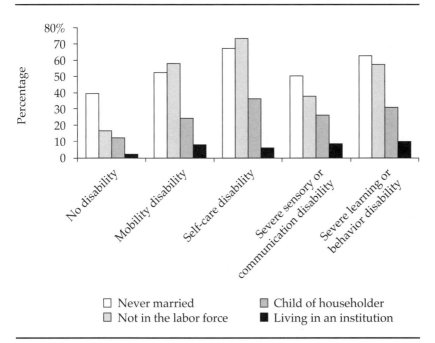

Never married          Child of householder
Not in the labor force          Living in an institution

*Source:* Author's calculations of data from the 2005 to 2009 American Community Survey
(Ruggles et al. 2010a).

sensory and communication limitations, and 46 percent of those with
cognitive limitations. Moreover, only 2 percent of adults ages twenty-
five to thirty-four who did not have disabilities were living in institutional settings (such as long-term-care facilities, group homes, or pris-
ons), compared to 3 percent of adults with mobility limitations, 6 percent
of adults with self-care limitations, and 8 percent of adults who had
cognitive and behavior limitations.

The transition of young persons with disabilities to adult roles and
to participation in the labor force is critical to the children's abilities to
lead adult lives. For all young persons, this can be a time fraught with
anxiety, as one learns adult social and behavioral skills and has to demonstrate work competence to find and keep good jobs. For parents of
young adults with multiple disabilities, one of the most helpful options
may be to enroll the child in a school-to-work program. Many children
with disabilities do manage to complete high school and transition suc-
cessfully to adult roles. However, there are many children who do not,
although these children may be partially independent (working at a

special job or living in a semi-independent setting), an accomplishment that accords some "adult" responsibilities. Children with more serious learning problems, behaviorally debilitating autism, or multiple disabilities are likelier to remain at home, fully dependent on their parents and with limited prospects for full participation in adult social roles.

Nonetheless, parents can be optimistic about the future. The parents of Peter, a seven-year-old with Down syndrome, say:

> Well it is hard to know at this stage what he is going to need. To a large extent it depends on how he feels. Some adults with Downs look forward to a group home, and some want to stay with Mom and Dad. We have relatives who have apartment buildings. He could be independent with people still having an eye on him. Our goal is to see how self-sufficient we can make him.

## Institutional Placement

Parents have a variety of reasons to place their children with disabilities in institutional residential settings. This often happens as their children reach adulthood—they may have troublesome behaviors that are more difficult to manage, and interventions by persons trained to promote acceptable behaviors can be effective. As adolescents with disabilities become adults, their parents also age and may become physically unable to continue their children's care at home. Sometimes, elderly parents want to place their children in a long-term institutional or supported living environment while they can support the transition, so that their children will be established in a caring environment after their own deaths.

Local and state governments are typically in charge of providing funding (beyond what Social Security Disability Insurance provides) for children and young adults with disabilities to live outside of the parental home in supported or supervised relationships, in group homes, or in long-term-care facilities. To receive these public supports, parents are generally required to put all decisions about the care of their child in the hands of the state. However, this can create conflicts between the tax authorities and program administrators who want to minimize the expense of such care, and parents who want their adult children to live in environments where they can thrive. One of the most effective tools families have to protect the interests of their children is to regularly visit the facilities in which the children live and to always attend the social worker's periodic case review.

When the social worker for Matt's case recommended that Matt be removed from Opportunity House, the group home he loved, to a less stimulating and less expensive facility, Matt's family appeared before their County Board of Supervisors. Often such decisions are made without the family present, but in this case, Matt and his family wanted to represent Matt's interests as they saw them. After the social worker gave his recommendation for the new placement, Matt's sister, Sally, who is a special education teacher, explained why the family wished to speak on behalf of Matt's interests. The Board of Supervisors was under no obligation to heed the family's wishes, but they were required to listen to their pleas. Sally relates what happened after the family gave its statement:

> Toward the end of the meeting, we whispered to Matt, "When the meeting is done, you can tell them thank you, if you want to." About five minutes later, the meeting ended. Sure enough, Matt stood up. But he did not give a thank you to the group. Instead he approached the ten people at the table and extended his hand to shake theirs. One by one, Matt went around the table, shaking hands and thanking them. As he shook the hand of the most difficult person, he also said, "It'll be okay. It'll be all right."

Matt was permitted to stay at Opportunity House.

Rhode Island has excellent support for the residential placement of persons with severe disabilities, but parents must decide to register their children for residential placement when they turn eighteen. Parents who wait beyond this age can only place their disabled children in residential settings when the parents can prove that they are themselves unable to provide their care. James's parents, who live in Rhode Island, had to make this choice. After much soul-searching, they decided to place James, who has severe autism, in a residential home when he reached age eighteen. James's father, Kevin, said this was extremely difficult, but he is convinced they made the right decision; he and his wife Naomi are delighted with the result. James is happy with his life—he shares supervised accommodations with other young adults with disabilities, has a job off-site sorting cans at a recycling center, has a small salary that he can spend, and enjoys a wide variety of social activities. His parents alternate weeks, visiting him at his residential home one week and bringing him to their home for an overnight stay in the next week and for all holidays. In this way, James is able to share in all major family events while having a degree of independence and autonomy that makes his life fulfilling.

Whatever the reasons children with disabilities are placed outside of the home, parents constantly worry about the safety of their children and whether they have a supportive and fulfilling living situation. This is dramatically illustrated in the case of Sandra, a twenty-three-year-old Hispanic woman with autism and severe mental retardation. Sandra went to live at a group home following episodes of violent behavior at home, including hitting herself, throwing things, and breaking furniture. One episode caused her to injure herself and resulted in a long hospital stay. Her mother was confident that she had found appropriate care when she enrolled Sandra in a day program at a private, state-licensed adult group home. It had worked well for Sandra, and her residence there appeared to be a perfect solution. However, things did not work out as her mother expected. Instead, Sandra was subjected to the abuse that is every parent's nightmare: "[Someone] pressed a hot curling iron against her chest, arms and feet on New Year's Eve."[3] Sandra now lives in another group home, but her mother still worries when she sees her daughter head out the door after her weekly visit home: "God knows how many times she was abused," her mother remarks.

How common is this problem? Data are difficult to come by, as state licensing agencies typically restrict public access to information about neglect and abuse in their facilities. Under Freedom of Information Act legislation, the *Providence Journal* was able to access this information and reported that "in a population of about 3,000 people getting services from private agencies in Rhode Island, including about 1,000 group-home residents, there were 11 rape allegations, [and] 31 allegations of assault that resulted in physical injury."[4]

Using Rhode Island crime statistics for the year 2000, one finds that the rate of rape allegations was 9.3 times higher among persons in the care of private agencies compared to the general population, and the rate of reported aggravated assault was 18.7 times higher.[5] While these calculations are crude, there exist many real dangers facing young adults with disabilities, particularly those with severe cognitive and communication disabilities who may be unable to articulate what has happened to them.

When young adults with disabilities cannot become residentially and economically self-sufficient and are not resident in institutions, they typically live as adults with their parents at home. For many parents this is a good arrangement. There are complications, however—one or both parents typically will need to work to provide economically for their child but may find they cannot safely leave the adult child with a disability alone at home. This is complicated by the scarcity of adult day programs for persons with disabilities.

Parents worry about the protection and well-being of their children when illness, old age, or death eventually prevents them from caring for their adult child with a disability. Peter's parents explain their worries about what will happen to their son with Down syndrome:

What I am worried about is other people taking advantage of him. I want him to know how to handle money. One thing that we are aware of but that we haven't yet done is estate planning. Learning how to protect himself from himself. I can see him now: "I made this really good friend, and he wants me to buy him a car."

# = Chapter 6 =

## The Lives of
## Brothers and Sisters

A  s seen in chapter 3, parents have a variety of options in decid-
ing whether to have another child when one of their children
already has a disability. Many parents whose first child is seriously disabled decide not to have another child because of the exceptional resource needs the family faces and their sense that it would not
be fair to have another child who could not be parented with as much
attention as he or she deserves. In cases where the disability of the child
is not as seriously limiting, parents may decide to have another child in
order to "complete their family." Some of these parents may also see a
younger brother or sister as someone who can help take care of their
disabled child once they are no longer able to do so. In other cases, it is
an older child who does not have a disability and a younger child who
does.

Families of children with disabilities certainly try to support their
children without disabilities as best they can; however, the problem
they face is that children with disabilities make great resource demands
on their families and these families often have lower incomes (exacerbated when the disability requires one parent—usually the mother—to
stay at home). Families in which a non-disabled child has a brother or
sister with a disability typically have different family dynamics than
families with no children with disabilities. The parents may be stressed
to provide all of the financial resources, the time, and the patience to
fully monitor their non-disabled children as well as their disabled
child. Associated with these different family dynamics is the fact that
the brothers and sisters without disabilities may end up with different
aspirations, life expectations, and behaviors than a non-disabled child
in a family in which no child has a disability.

This chapter examines this issue, although it is not an easy topic to
address with the information I have for this study. Because both children with and without disabilities move away from home beginning
around age eighteen, beyond age sixteen or so it is less certain that the
family structure of disability is correctly represented by household
membership in existing data sources. I have information about how the

parents at the Children's Rehabilitation Center (a total of fourteen families) describe their family relations when they have a child with disabilities and another child without. The National Health Interview Survey (NHIS) asks about all family members and, when pooled across five survey years, can be used to look at the health situations of children with siblings with disabilities compared to other children with siblings who are not disabled. Finally, the National Longitudinal Survey of Youth (NLSY) included as respondents all children in families who were twelve to sixteen years of age and able to complete an interview. This sibling sample lets me look at behavioral differences of children who have brothers and sisters with disabilities versus those who have brothers or sisters without disabilities; however, this comparison is not exact—for those adolescents who have brothers or sisters with disabilities who are younger than twelve or older than sixteen, the NLSY adolescents classified as having no sibling with a disability may, in some cases, have such a sibling.

## Interactions of Brothers and Sisters

Family life depends on how children without disabilities get along with their brothers or sisters with disabilities. Most parents at the Children's Rehabilitation Center say siblings of kids with disabilities act just like siblings would in any family—that is, sometimes harmoniously, sometimes combatively. Steve and Morgan have a brother named Jimmy who is fourteen years old and has cerebral palsy. Jimmy has difficulty with fine motor skills but can walk unsupported. Kelly, their mother, reports: "Like normal kids, sometimes they get along, other times they fight, other times they get along again. Usually they fight like typical brothers. 'Get out of my room!' Nothing different. It's like cerebral palsy isn't in my house."

### Resentment

Parents do express concern that the brothers or sisters will dislike all of the attention received by their sibling with a disability. Shannon says that her son Karl (age eleven) can be jealous of his disabled brother Louis (age fourteen), and this has gone on for years: "Karl complains, 'You spend more time with Louis than anybody. Louis gets everything; I get nothing.'" In the past two years, Louis, who is bigger, has been quite mean to Karl. "[Karl] has said on a number of occasions, 'I really hate Louis. I know that you think that I don't hate him, but I really hate him. If he would die, that would be okay with me.'" Shannon is so alarmed by the situation that she sought family counseling. But after just a few visits, the counselor said they were okay and did not need therapy. The problem continues to this day.

## Assistance with Personal Care

However, healthy children often help parents with the personal care needs of a disabled sibling. In the case of Vanessa (who has cerebral palsy) and her twin brother Alex, their mother reported, "He is . . . very, very protective of her. Very. Like, doesn't want her to get hurt. Doesn't want her to cry. . . . So, he's like the big brother." Mathew and Justin, the two older brothers of Scott, provide another example: "As the boys got older and more mature, you know if Scott needed help going outside in the winter, they'd help him put his jacket on. . . . If he fell outside, they'd pick him up. But they knock him down a lot, just by them playing with him, you know. But that was all par for the course."

## Emotional Advantages

At the same time, having a sibling with a disability creates an opportunity for the brothers and sisters to grow up with an understanding of the issues facing persons with disabilities in the community, and they are likely to have helpful attitudes toward others. This is apparent in the interviews with parents at the Children's Rehabilitation Center. For Jessica and Sarah, their brother David "has been a very positive influence . . . because it taught them to appreciate all the gifts that they've been given." The parents of Charlotte, the sister of Amelia, have watched the compassionate side of her personality develop: "One direction [Charlotte has] grown in is very empathetic. And nurturing. So that's what we saw come out when her sister was in treatment." Sister Kimberly and Sabrina, the healthy twin of Jacqueline, have grown in their acceptance of the disabilities of others: "I think, yeah, [Kimberly and Sabrina] definitely [deal] with disabilities a little bit easier. And maybe be a little bit nicer, or kinder."

In other cases, parents suggest that watching their siblings with a disability meet life challenges can strengthen the determination of their healthy children to do well in life. Margaret reports the improved sense of life course agency her son has developed because of having a brother with a disability:

> During football season, he injured his back and fractured his verte-brae. . . . When basketball season came, he wanted to play. And the doc-

tor said, "Well, the only way you can play is with the cast." . . . [His therapist] told me she had asked him if he found it difficult to do what he had to do with the body cast. You know, missing out. . . . And he said, "You know, when I see how my little brother has to struggle to move from one point to the other . . . this is nuthin'."

## Health Deficits

However, having a disabled brother or sister often is disadvantageous in aspects of children's lives in which family economic resources are important. The NHIS asks about shortcomings in medical care that are due to cost. The NHIS shows that the brothers and sisters of a disabled child are 40 percent more likely to have cost-related delays in receiving routine medical care. Because of cost, they are 15 percent more likely to go without needed prescription medications, 77 percent more likely to go without needed dental care (excluding orthodontic care), and 15 percent more likely to go without needed mental health care. These cost-related delays in care, taking into account family income, are indicative of the additional financial stresses on families raising children with disabilities and the extent to which managing the needs of a disabled child can limit investments in their healthy children.

The NHIS was used to address whether the overall health statuses of brothers and sisters differ when they have siblings with disabilities (these logistic regressions take into account the child's age and sex, race-ethnicity, family type, family size, parents' education, poverty status, and health insurance coverage). Brothers and sisters in a family in which another child has a disability are 30 percent more likely to miss ten or more days of school per year because of illness. Their relative risk of having a health status that is only fair or poor is three times higher (6 percent versus 2 percent for children in homes where there is no child with a disability). In addition, brothers and sisters of a child with a disability have a one-quarter increase in the odds that they have feelings of unhappiness, sadness, or depression compared to the brothers and sisters of healthy siblings.

The fact that these health disadvantages of growing up with a disabled sibling persist even when differences in family resources are taken into account suggests that at least part of the disadvantages encountered by these adolescents result from parents' decisions to allocate a greater share of limited resources to their children with disabilities. Of course, many parents will see this not as a decision but as what is simply necessary. There are, nonetheless, unfavorable consequences for the health care and education of their children without disabilities.

## Adolescent Behaviors

In other ways, siblings of children with disabilities are similar to those whose who brothers and sisters do not have disabilities. The NLSY shows that parents raising a child with a disability monitor where their non-disabled adolescent children are, who they are with, and what they are doing to the same extent as parents raising a child without a disabled sibling. The disability status of a sibling does not affect the quality or supportiveness of the parent-child relationship compared to children whose siblings do not have disabilities. This includes having closer relationships with their mothers than with their fathers, as do children with siblings without disabilities (in contrast to the closer relationships children with disabilities have with their fathers compared to their mothers).

Despite these major differences between the adolescent behaviors of children with and without disabilities, the brothers and sisters of children with disabilities are quite similar to other children during their own adolescence. Siblings of children with disabilities are only slightly more likely to engage in delinquent activities (1.9 on a 10-point scale) than children whose siblings are not disabled (1.5). Young people with siblings with disabilities are no more likely than young persons whose siblings do not have disabilities to use tobacco, alcohol, or marijuana. Running away by age eighteen is somewhat more common—25 percent of children whose siblings have disabilities run away, compared to 17 percent of children whose siblings have no disabilities. There are only trivial differences in the likelihood they are bullied—12 percent of children with a sibling with disability and 9 percent of those with a sibling without disabilities are bullied between twelve and eighteen years of age.

Compared to other sisters, girls growing up with a brother or sister with a disability engage in sexual behaviors that are higher risk but not as risky as those in which their disabled siblings engage. For girls whose siblings have disabilities, 44 percent of those who are sexually active had initial sexual intercourse when they were sixteen or younger, and 30 percent did not have a romantic relationship with their first partner. Girls who have siblings with disabilities have sex with a partner who is six or more years older 13 percent of the time compared to 8 percent of girls whose siblings do not have disabilities. These apparent differences in sexual behaviors between young persons whose siblings have disabilities and other young persons are largely explained by related family factors, but those family factors do not explain the much riskier adolescent behaviors of children who do have disabilities.

## Declining Involvement in Family Life

As they grow older and less dependent on parents for their own needs, most children become less involved in family life. This may be pronounced in the case of brothers and sisters who live in a family with a child with a disability. As one parent described, "[Sean, brother with disability] used to be closer with the oldest one [Stephanie]. I don't know what happened there. I guess boyfriend, you know, and then she's like out more than she's home." Indeed, brothers and sisters can "disappear" from the daily lives of their sibling with a disability as they make their own transition to adulthood. One parent described how this happened to her disabled son, David, when his sister finished high school: "You know, he used to go to his [sister's] basketball games. And at halftime he'd go and play and shoot baskets on the court. The parents were always in awe of him. . . . People would cheer for him . . . he just ate it all up, you know. He missed that after Jessica graduated."

## Transition to Adult Roles

Children growing up with a sibling with a disability attain less education than children who do not have disabled siblings. This examination of longer term consequences of having a sibling with a disability uses data from the annual NLSY surveys from 1997 to 2005. (All statistical models include controls for race-ethnicity, age and sex of the child, number of children under age eighteen living in the household, region of the country, and metropolitan residence.)

This is not because parents expect their children will get less education when another child has a disability. Children who have a sibling with a disability are themselves 16 percent less likely to think they will complete college, compared to children whose siblings do not have disabilities. And, unfortunately, the children's educational expectations are closer to what actually happens. While boys and girls who have a sibling with a disability are equally likely to complete high school, they are 31 percent less likely to enroll in college, than adolescents without disabled siblings. This difference in college enrollment is not related to poorer academic performances of the brothers and sisters of siblings with disabilities, as this statistical model also includes controls for the academic performance of the adolescents at the time they enter high school, as well as whether they are enrolled in remedial programs or have been held back one or more years in school.

Adolescents who have a brother or sister with a disability finish their schooling one year sooner than other adolescents, in part because of lower rates of college attendance. They also begin work and move away from home one year sooner.[1]

In short, adolescents who have a disabled brother or sister less often attend college since that may involve continued residence at home and parental investment, but they establish financial independence more quickly. This allows them to move out of their parents' homes at earlier ages than adolescents who do not have siblings with disabilities. This earlier transition to adult roles may result from their desire to avoid daily responsibilities for the care of their siblings with disabilities, but it may also be facilitated by the greater personal self-sufficiency that they have developed in their years of living with siblings with disabilities.

Thus, in many ways, the family lives of adolescent boys and girls with a sibling with a disability resemble those of other adolescents who have no siblings with disabilities. These adolescents do not engage in riskier behaviors, they get along with their parents equally well, and they are equally likely to complete high school. All of this is in contrast to the experiences of their siblings with disabilities, who more often engage in risky behaviors, get along less well with their mothers, and are less likely to complete high school. These findings offer strong support for the argument that it is not unmeasured family factors that cause the different experiences of children with disabilities (since their siblings from the same families do not have similar differences in experiences). In fact, most of the life course differences associated with a sibling with a disability relate to parental investments of money—children with a sibling with a disability are more likely to lack health care because of cost, more often have poor health, and are less likely to attend college. The economic stress on the family from the greater expenses and lowered incomes associated with raising a child with a disability affects all members of the family, including the brothers and sisters. Raising a child with a disability clearly is a family affair.

# === Chapter 7 ===

## Parents' Struggles for Disability Services

No study of the family consequences of children's disabilities would be complete without attention to parents' difficulties in negotiating and coordinating with service providers such as doctors, physical and occupational therapists, health care aides, teachers, counselors, and the panoply of other individuals who assist in the care of children with serious disabilities. These specialized services address medical conditions leading to disability and limitations in daily activities. Some children require medication and surgery to eliminate or alleviate disabling medical conditions, while others use medical devices and implants to treat medical conditions or to improve functional abilities. Still others may receive rehabilitation, education, and mental health or behavioral interventions. All of these specialized services depend on children's medical conditions and the extent to which their conditions are disabling in activities, but they also are fundamentally dependent on parents' resources, interactions, and advocacy with health and educational institutions.

Parents raising children with disabilities face many tough decisions about what services their children should receive. Parents are charged with enabling their children to participate in social roles and activities to the fullest extent possible. Yet these responsibilities cause considerable angst for many parents. Parents often have trouble getting accurate diagnoses or disability classifications. They struggle to get their children necessary and appropriate services from the medical care and educational systems. And they often second-guess the decisions they make about care and rehabilitation services, especially when the outcomes of those services are not as positive as they had hoped.

### Diagnosis

The difficulties parents have in getting appropriate treatment begin with the challenge of getting a timely and correct diagnosis for their child's disability. This is a recurrent theme among the parents interviewed at the Children's Rehabilitation Center. Shannon relates her frustrating experience trying to get a physician to seriously address her concerns about Louis:

> When he was in preschool [at age three], I kept saying to the doctor that I thought that something was wrong. Other kids could cut [with scissors] and hold a crayon, and he could not do these things. He had such a low frustration tolerance. But the doctor just kept saying, "Oh, Shannon, this is your first baby. Mothering is new to you." I wasn't being assertive because I thought I was being stupid.

After various tests in kindergarten and first grade, Shannon still did not have a diagnosis for Louis, although she was able to get some support from his school for learning limitations. Louis was in fifth grade before Shannon and her husband got a medical diagnosis of right hemisphere dysfunction associated with nonverbal learning disability and struggles with reading. This diagnosis guaranteed Louis access to all of the supports he needed. While Shannon was relieved to get an accurate diagnosis, she was then faced with the uncertain prospects for her son's future: "I was so petrified by what I read. It seemed like there was just no hope. There is all this terrible negative stuff because it is so new . . . people who write about it say that they are going to go through their lives miserable and unhappy, prone to commit suicide."

Adrian describes her frustration with getting a diagnosis for Francis, who has cerebral palsy:

> When he was in the incubator, and I kept asking the doctors and all the personnel in intensive care if there was something wrong with him. They kept telling me that he was just premature. . . . They needed to check him, but he needed to grow. And this is not what actually happened. Because you could see from the first days of his life an imperfection of his legs.

Adrian has an explanation for why Francis's cerebral palsy was not diagnosed until he was two years old: "You know the doctors don't want to expose themselves to a wrong diagnosis. Because then you can say, 'Oh, you told me that he would be able to do this and they didn't,' or did the opposite. So they try to wait."

## Misdiagnosis

Another problem parents face is misdiagnosis. Nathan developed at a normal pace and then experienced reversals. By age four, he could not raise his hands above his head. His pediatrician diagnosed him with muscular dystrophy. Nathan's mother described what happened next:

"And we ended up taking him to a neurologist the next day, who looked at him and said he was 99 percent sure it wasn't muscular dystrophy. And then sent blood work out and we ended up, I think we found out within a month what it is." (Nathan has MPS1, an enzyme deficiency that is a genetic disorder.)

Harry was unable to roll over by eight months. His parents brought him to a specialist who said that this delay was a consequence of having been born prematurely. But his mother Janet rejected this:

> I said, "You know, I don't think so." If I waited two or three more days it wouldn't be considered premature. . . . I said, "Ahh . . . you know, I just don't buy it" . . . because he was only four [pounds] seven [ounces] popping out of there. I was like nothin', you know. So [then] we went to a major university hospital and that's when they did the CAT scan. They said, "Yes, he had a stroke [in utero]." And they were like, "Oh my god."

## Parents' Decisions About Surgery

Nowhere are medical care decisions as stressful as in parents' decisions about surgical treatments. One issue for families is that once a decision is made for one surgical intervention, other surgeries may become necessary. For example, the mother of David, who has cerebral palsy, says: "He had metal plates on both hips, then he has his right foot straightened out. . . . This past September he has part two of the surgery. They removed the metal plates. They did a bilateral hamstring lengthening. They did a bilateral muscle transfer. And then they straightened out the left foot." After the initial surgery, then, there was no way to choose an alternative nonsurgical treatment for David.

The parents of Sadie followed another strategy. They did not like the initial physician's recommendations that Sadie receive multiple surgical interventions for the treatment of her cerebral palsy. Instead, they found another doctor who suggested a less invasive treatment strategy: "And that's when we learned that there's like a whole variety of people who think different things about what you should do with kids with spasticity in their leg. We ended up going with Dr. N and her plan. Um . . . just because it was less invasive."

## Case-Based and Individualized Strategies

The root of many parents' frustrations with the medical system is that parents and medical professionals often conceptualize a child's disability in quite different ways. Medical professionals typically view children through the lens of "cases." Their job is to diagnose a child's medical condition and look to see what treatments and interventions have been used for children with similar impairments. In doing this they often refer to "best practice" guidelines from professional associations. This is what we would expect health professionals to do. However, parents often worry that their child is being treated as "just another case" (Heimer 2001). Parents emphasize their child's individual characteristics—he or she is a "charmer," a "fighter," "tough," or especially "loving." Marilyn says this is the case with Erin:

> The doctor told us she may not walk [without] assistance. You know, that she may need a walker. Did not come true. They told us that she would not learn 'til very later on to ride a bike without trainers. She rides a bike without trainers. . . . She was determined she was going to learn how to jump rope. She jumps rope backwards faster than she does forward. So it's always like she finds her own way.

Some adjustments in the interactions between physicians and families would be helpful. Parents often feel that the medical care their children receive is not well explained, that doctors do not listen to their concerns, and that prescribed treatment plans may not be possible in their family. One-parent families, poor families, families with poor access to specialized care, families whose first language is not English, and families with different cultural heritages often are in this situation. While the usual emphasis in the care of children with disabilities is to get parents to adhere to treatment plans, in practice a better method might be family-centered care, which holds among its tenets that the perspectives and beliefs of families are valued and respected and that families may participate in decisions about medical care to the extent they choose. Adjusting treatment plans so they are realistic for parents raising children with disabilities will mean in practice that it is much more likely parents will provide their children with the medical care they need. Family-centered care enables parents to follow treatment protocols while emphasizing the individuality of their children and their potential for further improvement.

## Access to Medical Care

In the United States, access to care for the most disabling medical impairments requires some type of medical insurance coverage, either private or public. The percentage of uninsured children (5 to 6 percent) does not differ greatly by severity of disability. However, there are large social inequalities in the ability of parents to insure their children with disabilities (Davidoff 2004). According to an analysis of the National

Survey of Children with Special Health Care Needs (CSHCN), among children with severe disabilities whose families are in poverty and in which no parent has at least a high school diploma, 10 percent lack any form of health insurance. This compares with only 2 percent of children without health insurance among economically secure families in which at least one parent has a college degree. The probability that parents rely on public health insurance for their children increases dramatically by severity of disability, with 43 percent of children with severe disabilities covered by publicly provided insurance compared to 18 percent of children with mild disabilities. Children with severe disabilities who are from very poor families are privately insured in only 11 percent of cases, compared to 91 percent of children with severe disabilities in economically secure families.

As anyone whose loved ones have needed non-routine care knows, even when insurance is available there often are frustrations with coverage and other bureaucratic procedures. Josh's mother describes this situation when getting a new blood test that could help identify Josh's medical condition (and inform his parents about the risk that a new baby might have the same condition):

> I just actually had to, you know, call [my insurance] and try to get them to approve it . . . waiting on them to approve this test, like $1,200, we would have had to pay out of our own pocket . . . which we would have paid, we would have paid for it no matter what, but luckily . . . it took like three or four weeks and they approved it last Friday. And [we] had [the test] done Monday.

Like Josh's mother, many parents in the Children's Rehabilitation Center pointed to the routine difficulties of finding what treatments were covered, the need to get specialists or treatments pre-approved, the frequent loss of paperwork, the slowness in payment and reimbursement, and their inability to get a "straight answer."

However, the CSHCN shows that 83 percent of parents of children with special health care needs and no disabilities say their children's health insurance provides adequate coverage to see all necessary specialist providers, and 78 percent say that their insurance benefits meet their children's needs. However, only 38 percent of parents of children with severe disabilities report similar satisfaction with their current insurance. Even so, there is not a great deal of switching of health insurance companies; the parents seem to have realized from talking to other parents that while their insurance is not ideal, alternative insurance plans are likely to have many of the same issues.

Parents' fights with insurers are often heart-wrenching. One mother of a daughter with a severe connective tissue disorder told how she fought her insurance company over surgeries to enhance the quality of her daughter's life. The insurance company denied coverage because standard protocols were for the child's life to be compromised first, at which point the family would have lost their window of opportunity for the best outcome for restructuring the significant deformity of their daughter's rib cage. The mother filed a complaint with the state health department's insurance commissioner and also contacted her local state representatives, continually appealing this denial of services. Company documents that were revealed as a result of this complaint showed that the insurance company repeatedly referred to her in internal documents not by name but as "the irate mother." Following nine months of internal appeals and an external appeal paid for by the family, the decision was overturned and the insurance company was obligated to provide the surgeries necessary, but not without an emotional toll on the family.

## Quality Medical Care

The American Academy of Pediatrics developed the concept of a "medical home" to measure children's access to quality medical care (American Academy of Pediatrics 2002; Strickland et al. 2004). A child with a medical home has a usual source of care and health insurance, along with a health care provider who knows the child's overall health situation and provides "family-centered" care. Additionally, a child with a medical home receives referrals to specialists when necessary, can see those specialists, and has adequate coordination among multiple health care providers. The medical home concept provides a way to measure parents' success in obtaining quality medical care for their children.

Tabulations from the CSHCN show that three-fifths of children who have special health care needs but do not have disabilities have a medical home, compared to only two-fifths of children with severe disabilities (see figure 7.1). Parents who have higher levels of education and family income have more success in getting their children with severe disabilities a medical home. However, even among these families, less than half of parents of children with severe disabilities are able to provide their children with a medical home.

Only 27 percent of children with severe disabilities whose parents did not finish high school have a medical home. Families that are in poverty also find it difficult to secure a medical home for their severely disabled children (29 percent succeed). The CSHCN asked about each element of the medical home. The survey's findings show that parents

**Figure 7.1    Children Under Age Eighteen with Special Health Care Needs Who Have a Medical Home, by Disability Status**

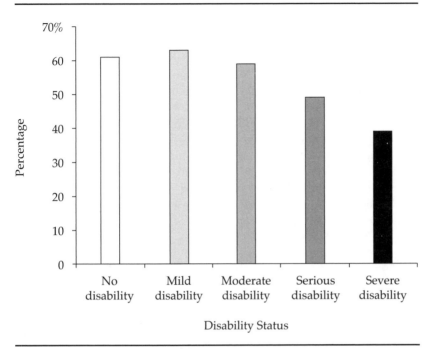

Disability Status

*Source:* Author's calculations based on the National Survey of Children with Special Health Care Needs (U.S. Department of Health and Human Services 2005/2006).
*Note:* Survey includes children who have special health care needs but who do not have disabilities.

of children with severe disabilities are about equally able to provide their children with a usual source of care (90 percent) and a knowledgeable doctor or nurse (90 percent) as parents of special health care needs children who do not have a disability. Parents of children with severe disabilities, compared to children with moderate disabilities, less often report that their health care providers spend enough time (78 percent versus 88 percent), listen to their concerns (82 percent versus 93 percent), or are sensitive to their cultural values (81 percent versus 92 percent).

The specialized services children receive from different providers are often disparate and uncoordinated; this obliges parents to become care coordinators and advocates for their children. This is illustrated by the interview with the mother of two daughters, Katie and Andrea. She is a special education teacher who can use her specialized knowledge to "work the system." She reported, "You need to know the medical laws, you need to know your coverage, you need to know every doctor they go to and what their specialty is, you need to keep up on the research."

## School Assistance

Unlike case-formulated medical treatment plans that rely on a standard protocol of how a particular disability presents itself clinically, school supports for a child with special education needs are individually designed. The idea that each child is a unique case who deserves individual diagnosis and specific treatments and interventions is codified in American law under the Individuals with Disabilities Education Act (IDEA). Under IDEA, an Individual Education Plan (IEP) is required in all public schools for every student with a disability who is found to qualify under federal and state criteria for special education. The IEP must be tailored to the individual student's needs as identified by the evaluation process and must help teachers and related service providers understand the student's disability and how the disability affects the learning process (U.S. Department of Education 2000).

Key considerations in developing an IEP include assessing the student in all areas related to the suspected types of disability, determining how to access the general curriculum, considering how the disability affects the student's learning, developing goals and objectives that make the biggest difference for the student, and ultimately choosing a placement in the least restrictive environment. Services for each student must be individually considered and recommended and should not depend on known or existing services. Each IEP must be designed to meet the specific needs of one student. Most important for families, the IEP must be designed to provide the child with Free Appropriate Public Education (FAPE) and must not be subject to financial charge.

School interventions can involve assistance with particular learning activities (such as reading or writing) as well as other specialized school activities. However, school-provided rehabilitation and enablement can also include services that are sometimes provided through health institutions or the community. These include occupational therapies (speech, communication, and small motor therapies), behavioral modification, personal assistance, and mental health services.

### Individual Education Plans

Schools can play an important role in legitimizing parents' concerns about their children's health conditions. For example, David was born prematurely but given a clean bill of health by his doctors. However, his mother reports that he did not develop as he should, as he failed to hold up his head and roll over until much later than other children. David's cerebral palsy was not diagnosed until he was eighteen months of age.

David's mother reports great frustration with failed diagnoses of David's hearing impairments:

> We noticed he didn't always hear us. . . . He'd jack up the volume on the TV and whatnot. But he'd hear some things but not hear others. We took him to be tested three times at a particular place. And each time they told us that he was fine.

But in kindergarten his teachers noted the same hearing problems. This time his mother got a referral to another audiology center: "And they found immediately that he had a profound hearing loss in one side. And significant in the other. So we finally got hearing aids . . . it was like a significant change in his life, to say the least."

Erin faces a contrasting situation. Cerebral palsy has mainly slowed her mobility, but she is not cognitively affected. Erin is a reminder that school assistance is only available when the disability limits learning. Her mother remarks:

> One thing that's a little bit disappointing to us is that she does not receive any services through our public education in the city that we live because her cognitive ability is so high and she tested so high that . . . they said PT and OT [physical therapy and occupational therapy] can stand alone. And it will not impact her ability to learn. And I totally disagree with that. Because if you have a child that is concentrating so much on their motor and keeping up, something else has to fall off the chart.

Even so, Erin spends so much time in school that her school experiences are critical:

> And we had a tough kindergarten teacher that really, you know one of the things that we had tried forever was to make Erin not feel different. But the [kindergarten] teacher . . . really brought a lot of attention to the fact that Erin wore the AFO [ankle-foot orthotic—a lightweight plastic ankle-foot brace] and how much work it was to get it on. So that was a struggle. It changed with a wonderful first grade teacher and a phenomenal second grade teacher.

The distinctions between PT and OT and special education that Erin's mother refers to are based in the differences between the medical model of disability and the educational model. The medical model, for example, looks at stretching, range of motion, and exercises completed. The educational model looks at whether the child is "functional" in the school environment in accomplishing fine and gross motor tasks. The educational model, for example, looks at whether a child can get from point A to point B in the building, can go through the lunch line, can use the pencil and scissors to accomplish classroom tasks, and can access the playground equipment. In many cases, the educational model will attempt to incorporate the medical model into the school-based services. However, if the school decides that the disability does not limit the child's ability to carry out age-appropriate tasks in school (as in Erin's case), the parents typically will need to get medical therapies elsewhere.

Although school-based special education programs are individualized, parents typically have more options in their dealings with the health care system than in their interactions with school programs. Parents with sufficient resources have the option to consult other health professionals, seeking the care providers with the diagnosis and treatment strategies they think are right for their child. Parents whose children are in public schools are less able to consult a variety of specialists with alternative special education recommendations; the schools define the services the child is eligible to receive and present the parents with a recommended IEP.

The formal consultation procedure schools employ in meetings with parents and the children about their IEPs can be an important way to involve the family in decisions about educational services for children with disabilities. These consultations also have the advantage of bringing together specialists from different areas of functioning and learning who can present a coherent, coordinated package of interventions. These advantages stand in sharp contrast to the chaotic situation that can ensue when multiple specialists recommend a variety of uncoordinated medical care interventions.

Despite the best intentions for IEP consultations, many parents find that they have limited ability to pick and choose from among the types of supports recommended by school officials. According to his mother Joan, Josh has tentatively been diagnosed as having a progressive and degenerative genetic disease. Josh is unable to speak, is unable to dress himself without assistance, is not toilet trained, and has mobility limitations. Joan describes the great frustrations getting necessary supports for Josh's education. After an early intervention program in which he received all of the supports he needed, Josh was enrolled in preschool at the age of three: "And we started preschool, and the whole year they kept trying to cut back on his therapies, and cut back . . . so it became a huge battle because, I mean, his needs are so straightforward and they were trying to cut back." Joan talks about a confrontational meeting with the school:

> So we had a meeting with the director of special education, and when she said that [the school refused additional services] I said, "Well, if that's the case then why do you work for the school department?" And at that point they threatened to adjourn the meeting and then they called in a mediator. They called me that day . . . from the State saying that a mediator was going to come in and discuss the matter, which we would have won, but it was just at that point there were so many hard feelings . . . so we decided to pull him from school, and we've been pursuing his therapies and home schooling at this point.

Minority and less educated parents have an especially difficult time influencing service decisions in an IEP. One study of teachers and children revealed the following:

> The educators thought they enthusiastically welcomed parental involvement and believed that their requests for parental involvement were neutral, technically efficient, and designed to promote higher levels of achievement. In reality, from a range of potential socioeconomic styles, they selected a narrow band of acceptable behaviors. They wanted parents not only to be positive and supportive but also to trust their judgments and assessments. (Lareau and Horvat 1999, 42)

Given this, it is likely that middle- and upper-class parents are able to draw on their superior educational skills, greater occupational flexibility, economic resources, and informed social networks to advocate for their child in discussions with educators about an IEP. Educators are more likely to view such parents as positive about and supportive of these IEPs. In contrast, many minority parents will approach the educators developing an IEP with the belief that there is a legacy of racial discrimination in schools (for example, the classification of black boys with disruptive behaviors as mentally retarded). Minority parents are more likely to display parental concern through criticism of educators, a behavior that educators may regard as unacceptable (Lareau and Horvat 1999).

Moreover, the development of an IEP can be so difficult that even some college-educated parents want an advocate in dealing with the schools. Gloria, who is a college graduate, felt this way when she was scheduled to go to the school to discuss the IEP of Emily (who has spina bifida):

> I was so upset [about Emily's treatment at the school]. . . . It was horrible for [Emily], and it was horrible for me. . . . I don't think a parent should

have to go to an IEP meeting at school by themselves. It's very intimidating. You walk in and there's four, five of them and there's you. . . . I called my cousin [who is] a college professor. And she does a lot of the IEPs. I called her and I said, "Could you come with me?" And she did. It was a three-hour long meeting. They were P.O.'d.

With careful planning by the school and parents, though, many parents find that school-based interventions can work extremely well, as they have for David. His mother described the balance between mainstreaming and special services:

PT, OT, speech, and adaptive phys ed [in school]. . . . So PT is once a week. OT is twice a week. Speech, I think, is twice a week at school . . . but some of those therapies are incorporated into the classroom work. He's not always pulled out for one-on-one. But other times with the speech teacher, whatever they're working on in the classroom and maybe something that she can do with him right in the [special education] class as part of the classroom work. . . . [In the integrated classroom] he was pulled out a little bit more. But you know, it seems to be working out okay. And teachers have always been great to try and to accommodate him in his special issues.

Schools are required to include transition planning in the IEP by the time students are fourteen years old and to be in receipt of transition services by the time they are sixteen. This transition planning revolves around services designed to help students with disabilities move into independent living, post-secondary education, and paid employment. This is a critical decision point for parents and children with disabilities, as the choices made will directly affect children's entry into adult roles.

Parents' choices of care begin with finding the right specialists to get an accurate diagnosis for their children. Parents need to identify possible treatment strategies and decide among them. For at least the next two decades they will be advocates for treatments that will enable their children to maximize their ability to participate in activities. This can require tense—and often unsuccessful—negotiations with health professionals, insurance companies, and schools for parents of children with disabilities compared to parents of other children with chronic health conditions but without disabilities. This constant interplay between advocating for their children in society and trying to maintain an emotionally stable and economically secure household raises particular challenges for family life, as we have seen.

# ═ Chapter 8 ═

## Conclusions

F AMILIES OF children with disabilities face a different set of challenges than do families whose children do not have disabilities. However, the lives of children with disabilities, their parents, and their siblings are not inferior. At a support group for parents of children with Down syndrome in 1995, anthropologist Rayna Rapp first heard a parable attributed to Emily Kingsley that metaphorically captures this truth:

> Imagine you have planned a vacation to Italy, to see the rose gardens of Florence. You are totally excited, you have read all the guidebooks, your suitcases are packed, and off you go. As the plane lands, the pilot announces, "Sorry, ladies and gentlemen, but this flight has been rerouted to the Netherlands." At first you are very upset: the vacation you dreamed about has been canceled. But you get off the plane, determined to make the best of it. And you gradually discover that the blue tulips of Holland are every bit as pretty as the red roses you hoped to see in Florence. They may not be as famous, but they are every bit as wonderful. You didn't get a red rose. But you got a blue tulip, and that's quite special, too. (Ginsburg and Rapp 1999, 197–98)

When I began this study of the family consequences of children's disabilities, I knew that I would learn about how children's disabilities affect their families. What I did not recognize at the time is how pervasive these consequences are and the extent to which raising a child with a disability affects the lives of mothers, fathers, brothers, and sisters.

## Shared Experiences Between Families

While the specifics of each child's situation vary, there were many common experiences among parents we interviewed at the Children's Rehabilitation Center: Parents initially encounter frustration when getting a medical diagnosis of their children's condition and when learning that there is uncertainty about the course of their children's medical impairments and how it will affect their daily activities. Parents are stressed by the unexpected challenges of raising a child with a disability and are much more likely to divorce in the first years of the child's life. As the child grows, there is the continuing need to advocate with health care and school institutions to get needed medical care, physical and occupational therapies, and special education. The parents' employment may be affected, particularly before their children enter school. For many families whose children are seriously or severely disabled, additional out-of-pocket expenses and lower incomes lead to financial insecurity. Such outcomes indicate the typical experiences of families; however, there is variation. Some families will experience only some of these outcomes, while other families will experience none. These outcomes depend in good part on the medical needs and abilities of children to engage in everyday life and to participate in age-appropriate activities.

Higher levels of parental education; strong earnings, income, and wealth; sound marriages; and personal resilience in dealing with life challenges all help to protect families from the more serious consequences of raising a child with a disability. So while these families face the same challenges in raising their children with disabilities as parents with fewer resources, they can use their greater resources to better manage their children's disabilities and care. Parents who are better educated more easily interact with health professionals and educators, who are more likely to respond with personalized care. Families with higher incomes can more easily pay the many out-of-pocket expenses for children with disabilities and, even if the mother leaves the labor force, can often avoid poverty, loss of their home, and basic economic insecurity. If the husband earns a sufficient income, it may facilitate the mother's purchase of child care in special facilities or by trained caregivers in the home. Other families find it positive that by providing full-time home care for their children with disabilities, the mother will also be a stay-at-home mother for all of their children. Nonetheless, even among parents who have the greatest social and economic resources, families who have children with severe disabilities are more likely to have more difficulties, though of somewhat smaller magnitude than peer families with less education and wealth.

It is critical to remember that most parents and families raising children with disabilities benefit in many ways, as the parable of the red roses and blue tulips suggests. These positive family outcomes are not measurable in population surveys (since the questions are not asked) but are revealed in interviews with families. If parents can get through the initial stresses of learning that their children have disabilities, their marriages are at least as strong as the marriages of other couples with children who do not have disabilities; in some cases, they are even stronger. The belief that children with disabilities are getting the best possible care is satisfying for parents and increases their confidence that they will be able to handle other issues as they arise. Parents also take great satisfaction in steps forward—even small steps—in their children's abilities.

Parents raising children with disabilities often have more family-centered lives, in which they, their children with disabilities, and their other children participate in more shared activities in the home. They are more likely to share experiences at meals, play games together, and watch television together. Religious faith often is strengthened, and houses of worship become more central as welcoming public spaces.

Older brothers and sisters help their younger siblings with disabilities more often and more intensively than would older siblings of children without disabilities. They develop caregiving skills that will help them with their own children and, likely, with parents, as they grow old and less able. They become more attuned to differences in abilities among others and are more understanding, helpful, and inclusive than young persons who do not have these experiences in their families. While I lack systematic information on the long-term employment of the siblings of disabled children, it is often thought (and my own observations and those of others suggest) that these brothers and sisters are more likely to go into helping professions, with specializations in medicine, education, social work, and advocacy for the disabled.

## Lessons Learned

While focused on families with children who have disabilities, this book has many lessons for social science research on the life course and family. It is a common social science method to examine specific population groups in order to understand the norms and conventions that are central to groups, communities, and social institutions. For example, studies of same-sex and cohabiting unions have helped social scientists better understand the dynamics of heterosexual unions, including how such unions are formed; how people select their mates; and the characteristics common to marriage or union stability, separation, and divorce. Similarly, studies of family life will be enhanced by learning whether parental stress in a household is due to the parents' own characteristics and behaviors, the usual kinds of family concerns and financial worries, or the birth and raising of children with disabilities. Understanding how those stresses affect marital dissolution and decisions regarding additional childbearing among couples parenting a child with a disability is likewise important for a broader understanding of family life, union formation, and fertility intentions.

Social scientists often also study support networks. This book argues that sociologists should consider the kinds of support parents receive when that support is not straightforward and of the usual sort—

for example, who helps with child care when a child is physically dependent or has outbursts of "unacceptable" behavior? Why are some extended family members helpful and others not? Do unhelpful kin avoid contact with the family? Is the extended family more likely to help financially when a couple's economic needs are not due to bad decisions or bad luck, but instead to the extraordinary challenges of raising children with disabilities? Or does kin support continue or diminish when the financial needs are too great for it to make much difference? The inclusion of families with children with disabilities in family research will open new windows on support networks.

Economists and other social scientists are interested in "inter vivos transfers"; that is, how parents decide to allocate resources between their own consumption and savings on the one hand and transfers of resources to their living children on the other (Cox and Rank 1992). The exchange theory suggests that parents invest in their living children to support closer contact and better relations with their children now, in anticipation of financial reciprocity as the parents grow older and as their personal care and financial needs become greater. By investing more heavily in their children and grandchildren when they are young, parents can raise the earnings capacity of children and grandchildren so that the children will need to sacrifice less to help them in old age. In this theory, parents invest in those children who are most likely to profit from that aid—for example, supporting college education for children who go to college and not giving comparable financial resources for the activities of other children who do not go to college. They also invest more resources in their children they think are most likely to reciprocate assistance to them in old age. If it is not possible to tell which child will benefit the most from resource transfer, or which of the children is more likely to assist them in old age, parents will invest equally in their children.

In contrast, the altruistic model posits that parents care about the well-being of their progeny and reap satisfaction from giving them resources. Under this model, parents will expect to initially transfer equal resources to their children but will give additional assistance to the children who need it the most. That is, they will attempt to help children with fewer endowments by giving them more support. Studies of inter vivos transfers in families in which some children have disabilities and other children do not offer a unique opportunity to examine these alternative theories. The results in this book suggest that the support parents provide to their disabled children reduces the support their children without disabilities would otherwise be expected to receive.

General sociological studies of the life course of young people as they transition from adolescence to adulthood are decidedly inferior if they neglect to include young people with disabilities. While health conditions and cognitive ability are sometimes included in studies of the life course, there is rarely any attention to limitations in the ability of young persons to do activities of daily life and participate in key adolescent and adult roles. This is partly a practical consideration, since children with the most serious cognitive disabilities are not able to respond to complex survey questions, but the analysis here using the National Longitudinal Survey of Youth demonstrates that the life courses of children with disabilities who are cognitively able to participate in a survey, along with the life courses of their brothers and sisters, are critical in understanding departures from the "normative life course." This shows that children with many disabilities often are able to participate in population surveys and that their life courses are different from those of other young people without disabilities. That is, the data is there but too frequently ignored in research on the life courses of children, adolescents, and young adults.

Understanding how parents and children formulate alternative life plans when they are not able to take the usual pathways will increase insight into the roles of parent support and children's agency in the transition to adulthood. The parental resources and family nurturing that adolescents rely on for a successful transition to adult life are often stretched when families have children with disabilities. Just as family size is typically considered in statistical models of the life course, the disability status of young persons being studied and disabilities in the family should be specified. This will provide better insights into why some young persons have alternative pathways to adulthood and what the results of these alternative pathways are. (In statistical language, inclusion of disability information reduces omitted variable bias.)

Social workers and clinical family psychologists will also benefit from this research. Intake forms for new patients should ask not only about who is in the family, but whether any children in the family are disabled. Interventions that rely greatly on parents' involvement (for example, working with obese children to adjust their diets) will be much less effective if the parents need to devote more of their time and resources to helping disabled brothers or sisters. If medications or other supports are needed for children without disabilities, health professionals need to find out whether a disabled child with considerable medical costs will keep the parents from purchasing these.

Educators at siblings' schools should be informed, as well. While siblings of children with disabilities should not be present in the development of individual education plans, special educators in schools should meet more formally with the other children in the family, with parents present, to explain the nature of their sibling's disability, the plans for special education supports, and the goals of special education and to include them in discussions of how they can be supportive of their siblings and of their families. Finally, it is essential that welfare eligibility criteria consider the family obligations for the care of a child with a disability to determine whether a mother should work.

Parents and parent support groups can also benefit from this study. Instead of relying on interpersonal contacts between parents, support groups could help organize child care exchanges so that mothers can have some relief from constant caregiving and parents can experience some daytime activities or nights out and in return provide this support to other families. This would help strengthen the bonds between parents in similar situations. Support groups could also organize activities for the brothers and sisters of children with disabilities. This could not only improve the information available to them but could, if structured around social activities, enable them to interact with other young people in similar situations.

## Health Care Policy Effects and Recommendations

The 2010 national health care reform plan was especially important for families of children with disabilities. The more generous rules for financial qualification for Medicaid will help more families get public insurance to meet their children's needs. This is especially important since necessary and appropriate care is now mandated under Medicaid for children whose first health screenings indicate that they have a chronic health condition or a disability. On the private insurance side, insurers are no longer permitted to deny coverage to children with disabilities because the overall insurance expenditure caps have been reached. Private insurers are no longer able to deny family coverage, or exclude children from family coverage, if children have a pre-existing condition. This provision means that parents will be able to move more readily from one employer to another, including to a position with more flexible work hours or to work in the home. The extension to age twenty-five of children's medical coverage under family plans is also of great assistance to families raising children with disabilities. Whatever changes, if any, are made to the American health care system in the future, it is essential that these crucial benefits for families of children with disabilities remain in place.

If I had written this book three years ago, I would have made wide-ranging policy recommendations for government programs in support of the families of children with disabilities. In the midst of discussions about draconian budget cuts in social welfare programs, this is not the time to make such recommendations; they would simply be unrealistic. Nonetheless, budgets for programs that assist families of children with disabilities should not be cut back or eliminated. There are some other things governments could do that would help families of children with disabilities. The minimum medical expenditures relative to income that must now be met before deducting medical expenses from taxable income could be lowered when children's medical conditions or disabilities increase the costs of care. The standard income tax deduction for children could be increased if children in the family have serious medical conditions or severe disabilities. In any case, the standard child deduction should be extended for children with disabilities who are college age and not enrolled. This would be helpful for parents who face extraordinary non-medical expenses to support their children at home (for example, house modifications, special vans, or special foods).

In conclusion, I hope that this book has assured families of children with disabilities that many of the difficulties they encounter are not unique to them, so that they are better prepared to deal with medical and education service providers and can gain knowledge from the experiences and actions other parents. I have also aimed to enlighten medical professionals, social workers, clinical and family psychologists, and educators of the special situations of families of children with disabilities and the implications for family issues and for the care of other children. It is essential that the brothers and sisters of children with disabilities be more formally involved, and more often included, in discussions of their siblings' special needs.

Finally, my goal has been to expand social science knowledge by noting insights gained from the study of families of children with disabilities. In so doing, I hope that I have made the case that sociologists should consider how children's disabilities affect the life courses of their entire families and how support networks and intergenerational assistance differ in these families. This study represents the culmination of my fifteen years of scholarship on families of children with disabilities. I hope that all readers will have gained an understanding of the extraordinary efforts of these families and the fact that we as individuals, families, organizations, and communities should do what we can to support them in the many challenges they face.

# ═ Notes ═

## Chapter 2

1. This chapter is coauthored with Michael E. Msall and Roger C. Avery.
2. In 2007, the WHO expanded this model and released the International Classification of Functioning, Disability and Health for Children and Youth (ICF–CY). It was created especially for children in order to account for the specific and unique aspects of disability in childhood. For many children, disability is explained in the context of delays, deviations, and variations in growth or development (Hogan and Park 2000). In population surveys, parents are seldom asked about developmental delays; indeed, in many of the surveys the same instruments are used to measure child and adult disability. The history of developmental delays in children with diagnosed disabilities is captured in the interviews at the Children's Rehabilitation Center. The interviews show that the family consequences of initial developmental delays and subsequently identified functional disabilities are quite similar. For these reasons I use the WHO's ICF.
3. For more information on the National Survey of Family Growth (NSFG), visit http://www.cdc.gov/nchs/nsfg.htm.
4. For more information on the National Health Interview Survey (NHIS), visit http://www.cdc.gov/nchs/nhis.htm.
5. For more information on the National Health Interview Survey on Disability (NHISD), visit http://www.cdc.gov/nchs/nhis/nhis_disability.htm.
6. For more information on the National Survey of Children with Special Health Care Needs (CSHCN), visit http://www.cdc.gov/nchs/slaits/cshcn.htm.
7. For more information on the National Survey of Children's Health (NSCH), visit http://www.cdc.gov/nchs/slaits/nsch.htm.
8. For more information on the National Longitudinal Survey of Youth (NLSY), visit http://www.bls.gov/nls/nlsy97.htm.
9. For more information on the National Longitudinal Transition Study of Special Education Students (NLTS), visit http://www.nlts2.org.

## Chapter 3

1. This chapter is coauthored with Frances K. Goldscheider.

## Chapter 5

1. This chapter is coauthored with Carrie L. Shandra.

2. This difference is based on ordinary least squares regression models of parents' expectations in the first wave of the NLSY. These models included controls for number of parents in the household, family income, parents' education, family size, sex and race-ethnicity of the child, and educational characteristics (grades in eighth grade, remedial education, days absent from school, repeated grade, parents' educational involvement, and percentage of peers who plan to attend college).

3. Mider, Zachary R., "Sandra picks at her shirt, looks at her mother; 'God knows, how many times she was abused,' says Gladys T. Ocasio," *The Providence Sunday Journal*, June 5, 2005, A1, A13.

4. Mider, Zachary R., "Sandra picks at her shirt, looks at her mother; 'God knows, how many times she was abused,' says Gladys T. Ocasio," *The Providence Sunday Journal*, June 5, 2005, A1, A13.

5. Available at: http://www.disastercenter.com/crime/ricrime.htm.

## Chapter 6

1. Monthly data on school, work, and residence from 1997 to 2005 in the NLSY allows for the description of the ages at which young persons with and without siblings with disabilities complete their highest grade of school, begin their first full-time job, and first become residentially independent from their parents. Kaplan-Meyer survival estimates were used to obtain the median age at these transitions, taking into account the experience of the entire sample—both those who had made the transitions and those who had not.

# ═ References ═

American Academy of Pediatrics, Medical Home Initiatives for Children with Special Needs Project Advisory Committee. 2002. "The Medical Home." *Pediatrics* 110(July 1): 184–86.

Blackorby, Jose, and Mary Wagner. 1996. "Longitudinal Postschool Outcomes of Youth with Disabilities: Findings from the National Longitudinal Transition Study." *Exceptional Children* 62(5): 399–413.

Brandon, Peter D. 2000. "An Analysis of Kin-Provided Child Care in the Context of Intrafamily Exchanges: Linking Components of Family Support for Parents Raising Young Children." *American Journal of Economics and Sociology* 59(2): 191–216.

Brandon, Peter D., Sandra Hofferth, and Dennis P. Hogan. 2008. "Do Disabilities in Former TANF Families Hasten Their Return to Welfare?" *Social Science Research* 37(2): 530–43.

Brandon, Peter D., and Dennis P. Hogan. 2004. "Impediments to Mothers Leaving Welfare: The Role of Maternal and Child Disability." *Population Research and Policy Review* 23(4): 419–36.

Brooks-Gunn, Jeanne, Greg J. Duncan, Pamela Kato Klebanov, and Naomi Sealand. 1993. "Do Neighborhoods Influence Child and Adolescent Development?" *American Journal of Sociology* 99(2): 353–95.

Centers for Disease Control and Prevention. 1995. *National Health Interview Survey on Disability* (NHISD). Available at: http://www.cdc.gov/nchs/nhis/nhis_disability.htm (accessed February 24, 2012).

Cox, Donald, and Mark R. Rank. 1992. "Inter-Vivos Transfers and Intergenerational Exchange." *The Review of Economics and Statistics* 74(2): 305–14.

Davidoff, Amy J. 2004. "Insurance for Children with Special Health Care Needs: Patterns of Coverage and Burden on Families to Provide Adequate Insurance." *Pediatrics* 114(August 1): 394–403.

Elder, Glen H. Jr., Monica Kirpatrick Johnson, and Robert Crosnoe. 2003. "The Emergence and Development of Life Course Theory." In *Handbook of the Life Course*, edited by Jeylan T. Mortimer and Michael J. Shanahan. New York: Kluwer Academic/Plenum Publishers.

Engle, Patrice L., and Maureen M. Black. 2008. "The Effect of Poverty on Child Development and Educational Outcomes." *Annals of the New York Academy of Sciences* 1136(1): 243–56.

Ginsburg, Faye, and Rayna Rapp. 1999. "Fetal Reflections: Confessions of Two Feminist Anthropologists as Mutual Informants." In *The Fetal Imperative*, edited by Meredith Michaels and Lynn Marie Morgan. Philadelphia: University of Pennsylvania Press.

Guendelman, Sylvia, Roberta Wyn, and Yi-Wen Tsai. 2000. "Children of Working Low-Income Families in California: Does Parental Work Benefit Children's Insurance Status, Access, and Utilization of Primary Health Care?" *Health Services Research* 35(2): 417–41.

Heimer, Carol A. 2001. "Cases and Biographies: An Essay on Routinization and the Nature of Comparison." *Annual Review of Sociology* 27: 47–76.

Hogan, Dennis P., and Daniel Lichter. 1995. "The Living Arrangements and Welfare of Children and Youth." In *State of the Union: America in the 1990s*, vol. 2, *Social Trends*, edited by Reynolds Farley. New York: Russell Sage Foundation.

Hogan, Dennis P., and Michael Msall. 2007. "Key Indicators of Health and Safety: Infancy, Pre-School, Grade School, and Middle School." In *Key Indicators of Child and Youth Well-Being: Completing the Picture*, edited by Brett Brown. Mahwah, N.J.: Lawrence Erlbaum Associates.

Hogan, Dennis P., Michael E. Msall, and Julia A. Rivera Drew. 2008. "Developmental Epidemiology of Mental Retardation and Developmental Disability." *International Review of Research in Mental Retardation* 33: 213–45.

Hogan, Dennis P., Michael E. Msall, Michelle L. Rogers, and Roger C. Avery. 1997. "Improved Disability Population Estimates of Functional Limitation Among American Children Aged 5–17." *Maternal and Child Health Journal* 1(4): 203–16.

Hogan, Dennis P., and Jennifer M. Park. 2000. "Family Factors and Social Support in the Developmental Outcomes of Very Low-Birth Weight Children." *Clinics in Perinatology* 27(2): 433–59.

Hogan, Dennis P., Jennifer M. Park, and Kelly Holder. 2004. "The Measurement of Learning Disability in Population-Based Survey Research." Report submitted to the Assistant Secretary for Planning and Evaluation, National Institutes of Health, New York.

Lareau, Annette, and Erin McNamara Horvat. 1999. "Moments of Social Inclusion and Exclusion: Race, Class, and Cultural Capital in Family-School Relationships." *Sociology of Education* 72(1): 37–53.

Lyon, G. Reid. 1996. "Learning Disabilities." *The Future of Children* 6(1): 55–76.

MacInnes, Maryhelen D. 2008. "One's Enough for Now: Children, Disability, and the Subsequent Childbearing of Mothers." *Journal of Marriage and Family* 70(3): 758–71.

Moore, Kristen (Child Trends, Inc. and Center for Human Resource Research). 1999. *Family Processes and Adolescent Outcome Measures* [NLSY97 Codebook Supplement, Main File Round 1, Appendix 9]. Ohio State University: Center for Human Resource Research.

Msall, Michael E., Roger C. Avery, Michelle R. Tremont, Julie C. Lima, Michelle L. Rogers, and Dennis P. Hogan. 2003. "Functional Disability and School Activity Limitations in 41300 School-Age Children: Relationship to Medical Impairments." *Pediatrics* 111(March 1): 548–53.

Newacheck, Paul W., Bonnie Strickland, Jack P. Shonkoff, James M. Perrin,

Merle McPherson, Margaret McManus, Cassie Lauver, Harriette B. Fox, and Polly Arango. 1998. "An Epidemiologic Profile of Children with Special Health Care Needs." *Pediatrics* 102(July 1): 117–23.

Park, Jennifer M., Dennis P. Hogan, and Maryhelen D'Ottavi. 2004. "Grandparenting Children with Special Needs." *Annual Review of Gerontology & Geriatrics* 24(1): 120–49.

Park, Jennifer M., Dennis P. Hogan, and Frances K. Goldscheider. 2003. "Child Disability and Mothers' Tubal Ligation." *Perspectives on Sexual and Reproductive Health* 35(3): 138–43.

Presser, Harriet B. 2003. *Working in a 24/7 Economy: Challenges for American Families*. New York: Russell Sage Foundation.

Ruggles, Steven, J. Trent Alexander, Katie Genadek, Ronald Goeken, Matthew B. Schroeder, and Matthew Sobek. 2010a. *American Community Survey, Integrated Public-Use Microdata Series: Version 5.0* [Machine-readable database]. Minneapolis: University of Minnesota.

———. 2010b. *United States Census 2000, Integrated Public-Use Microdata Series: Version 5.0* [Machine-readable database]. Minneapolis: University of Minnesota.

Shandra, Carrie L., and Dennis P. Hogan. 2008. "School-to-Work Program Participation and the Post High School Employment of Young Adults with Disabilities." *Journal of Vocational Rehabilitation* 29(2): 117–30.

———. 2009. "The Educational Attainment Process Among Adolescents with Disabilities and Children of Parents with Disabilities." *International Journal of Disability, Development and Education* 56(4): 363–79.

Simeonsson, Rune J., Donald J. Lollar, Joseph Hollowell, and Mike Adams. 2000. "Revision of the International Classification of Impairments, Disabilities, and Handicaps: Developmental Issues." *Journal of Clinical Epidemiology* 53(2): 113–24.

Strickland, Bonnie, Merle McPherson, Gloria Weissman, Peter Van Dyck, Zhihuan J. Huang, and Paul Newacheck. 2004. "Access to the Medical Home: Results from the National Survey of Children with Special Health Care Needs." *Pediatrics* 113(May 1): 1485–92.

U.S. Bureau of Labor Statistics. 1997. *National Longitudinal Survey of Youth, 1997 Cohort*. Washington: U.S. Department of Labor, Bureau of Labor Statistics.

U.S. Department of Education. 2000. *A Guide to the Individualized Education Program*. Available at: http://ed.gov/parents/needs/speced/iepguide/index.html (accessed January 12, 2012).

U.S. Department of Health and Human Services. 2003. *National Survey of Children's Health*. Maternal and Child Health Bureau, U.S. Department of Health and Human Services, Human Resources and Services Administration. Available at: http://www.cdc.gov/nchs/nsfg.htm (accessed January 12, 2012).

———. 2005/2006. *National Survey of Children with Special Health Care Needs*. Washington: Maternal and Child Health Bureau, U.S. Department of Health and Human Services, Human Resources and Services Administration.

Van Dyck, Peter C., Merle McPherson, Bonnie B. Strickland, Kerry Nesseler,

Stephen J. Blumberg, Marcie L. Cynamon, and Paul W. Newacheck. 2002. "The National Survey of Children with Special Health Care Needs." *Ambulatory Pediatrics* 2(1): 29–37.

Wells, Thomas, Gary D. Sandefur, and Dennis P. Hogan. 2004. "What Happens After the High School Years Among Young Persons with Disabilities?" *Social Forces* 82(2): 803–32.

World Health Organization. 2001. *International Classification of Functioning, Disability and Health.* Geneva: World Health Organization.

# ═ Index ═